SONGS FOR THE BRIDE

STUDIES IN ORIENTAL CULTURE, NUMBER 20

COLUMBIA UNIVERSITY

BIHAR IN 1940

N E P A L

CHAMPARAN

Motihari

Gogra R.

Gandak R.

Madhubani

MUZAFFARPUR   D.

SARAN   M.   DARBHANGA

U. P.   Chapra   M I T H I L A   PURNEA

Bankipore   Purnea

Arrah   Patna

B H O J   Ganges R.

SHAHABAD   P A T N A   M.   B.

MAGADHA   MONGHYR   BHAGALPUR

Son R.   GAYA

Rohtas   G.   SANTAL PARGANAS

B I H A R

PALAMAU   HAZARIBAGH   Dumka

Daltonganj   Hazaribagh

C H O T A   N A G P U R   Damodar R.

Ormanjhi

Ranchi   Hooghly R.

Gumla   Purulia

C. P.   RANCHI   MANBHUM

B E N G A L

Calcutta

Chaibasa   Subarnarekha R.

SINGHBHUM

P.A.S./'83   O R I S S A

Legend

Boundaries : National ⬤●●▬ , Provincial ⬤▬●▬ , District ········
Administrative Hq. : Provincial ● ,District ● .   Other towns (selected)●
(Names of district hq. are same as those of district unless otherwise shown.)
Names of localities prominently associated with William Archer are underlined.

SONGS FOR THE BRIDE

Wedding Rites of Rural India

WILLIAM G. ARCHER

EDITED BY

BARBARA STOLER MILLER

AND

MILDRED ARCHER

COLUMBIA UNIVERSITY PRESS

NEW YORK

UNESCO COLLECTION OF REPRESENTATIVE WORKS

Indian Series

This book has been accepted in the translations collection of the United Nations Educational, Scientific and Cultural Organization (UNESCO).

The editors would like to thank Philip A. Schwartzberg for preparing the map "Bihar in 1940"; they would also like to thank The India Office Library and Records, London, for permission to use all photos of Indian art that appear in the book.

Library of Congress Cataloging in Publication Data

Archer, W. G. (William George), 1907–
    Songs for the bride.

    (Studies in Oriental culture ; no. 20)
    Bibliography: p.
    Includes marriage songs in Bhojpuri (roman) and English.
        1. Marriage customs and rites—India—Bihar.
    2. Folk-songs, Bhojpuri—Translations into English.
    3. English poetry—Translations from Bhojpuri.
    4. Folk-songs, Bhojpuri—Texts.   5. Bihar (India)—
    Social life and customs.   I. Miller, Barbara Stoler.
    II. Archer, Mildred.   III. Title.   IV. Series.
    GT2776.A3B542   1985   392'.5'095412   84-23029
    ISBN 0-231-05918-3

Columbia University Press
New York   Guildford, Surrey

Printed in the United States of America
c 10 9 8 7 6 5 4 3 2

Clothbound editions of Columbia University Press books
are Smyth-sewn and printed on permanent and
durable acid-free paper.

CONTENTS

FOREWORD

William George Archer began his lifelong involvement with India as a member of the Indian Civil Service in Bihar in 1931. His scholarly work profoundly changed previous conceptions of Indian folk art and poetry, as well as of miniature painting.

During the sixteen years he lived and worked in India, his keen eye and his sensitivity to oral poetry led him to discover art where other educated men could neither see nor hear it. The rich collections of visual and verbal material he made occupied him even after he left India and returned to England to become Keeper of the Indian Section of the Victoria and Albert Museum. Although his later work focused on the Museum's collection of Indian miniature paintings, he continued to revise and analyze his unpublished studies of Indian folk culture.

The current work, begun in 1940 and drafted into a manuscript in 1944, was a project which he was planning to revise at the time of his death in March 1979. When Mildred Archer showed the manuscript to me in the summer of 1982, I agreed to help her edit it for publication.[1] As is characteristic of each of Archer's studies of folk poetry, these songs of the Kayasth women of the former Shahabad district of Bihar (since 1961 the Arrah district) are carefully placed within their regional, social, and ritual contexts.

Archer's ability to respond to Indian folk art and poetry is understandable in light of his earlier fascination with African sculpture and the abstract forms of twentieth-century art. He was especially drawn to the poems of T. S. Eliot, and to the paintings of Picasso, Cézanne, Miro, and the Surrealists. Although he read history and

economics at Emmanuel College, Cambridge, art and poetry were his
passion. They continued to shape his life in India, where he held
administrative posts in various districts of Bihar province from 1931
to 1946 and then served for almost two years in the Naga Hills of
Assam before returning to England in 1948.

In each of his posts Archer learned what he could of the local
customs, rituals, dialects, and tribal languages. His first encounter
with village art occurred at Christmas time in 1931, on a tiger shoot
in the area of Rohtas, in Shahabad district. He was repelled by killing tigers but thrilled by the strange stone and wooden figures he
saw standing in pairs in villages throughout the area, with their sim-
ilarities to African, Celtic, and modern European sculptural forms.
The images centered on the cult of the cattle god Bir Kuar, who was
worshiped by the Ahir caste of the region to protect their cattle
from tigers. In 1935 Archer returned to photograph images in different villages and to record the rituals and oral literature associated
with them. In 1939 he spent five months on leave in the area to
finish the work, which was published in *The Vertical Man: A Study
of Primitive Indian Sculpture*.

In 1933 and 1934 Archer was posted to Madhubani in Darbhanga
district as a Subdivisional Officer. During these years he developed
a taste for Indian folk painting and began to collect examples. On a
trip to Calcutta with his friend Humayun Kabir, he purchased a few
Kalighat paintings from the last of the Kalighat artists and from the
collection of the Bengali artist Mukul Dey. He bought a group of old
Jagannath paintings when he visited Puri. Like the Kalighat paintings they had been made for sale to pilgrims at the temples. These
early purchases formed the nucleus of a large personal collection,
which was later acquired by the India Office Library, where it was
catalogued by Mildred Archer in the volume *Indian Popular Painting*.[2]

His great discovery came when a severe earthquake struck Bihar
in March 1934. In the course of relief work, he saw superb mural
paintings inside the broken mud houses of Maithil Brahmins and
Kayasths in the Madhubani subdivision. Although these intricately

stylized, brilliantly colored murals must have belonged to an old Maithil tradition, they were virtually unknown outside the region. He later found that the practice extended eastwards to Purnea district.

Archer first became aware of tribal poetry during the years from 1934 to 1937, when posted as Joint Magistrate and Deputy Collector in charge of the Gumla subdivision in Chota Nagpur. Here he was intrigued by the presence of singing whenever the Uraons performed dancing, marriage rituals, or crop cultivation. While camping in Or-manji near Ranchi during his settlement training in 1932, he had noticed that the Uraon men and women sang as they went about their work or danced at night. When he went to Gumla, he began to learn the Uraon language and decided to record the texts of the songs. He encouraged his subordinates to collect and write down the words of songs whenever they stopped in villages. He himself recorded Uraon marriage dialogues and riddles within the region. He also kept de-tailed notes relating the songs to the social activities with which they were connected. The study confirmed the importance of dance and its accompanying poetry to the social transactions of Uraon culture.

The translations and analyses of this material were published in 1940 in a volume entitled *The Blue Grove,* with a foreword by Arthur Waley, who saw the manuscript and was struck by the similarity of imagery between this Indian tribal poetry and early Chinese poetry. The texts of 2,600 Uraon songs and 440 Uraon riddles, edited with F. Hahn and Daramdas Lakra, were published in Bihar in 1941 as *Lil Khora Khekhel.* More English versions of the songs were later published in *The Dove and the Leopard.* The vigor with which Archer collected, recorded, classified, and critically analyzed this material was as noteworthy as the literary quality of his translations.

A great opportunity for Archer to extend his studies of rural paint-ing and poetry came when he was posted to Hazaribagh as Provincial Census Superintendent in 1939. While setting up census procedures he was able to tour the whole province and study the various tribes and castes whom he had encountered during previous assignments. It was during this period that he revisited the Madhubani area and

collected the aide-mémoire designs for wall paintings that are illustrated here. He was also able to organize the collection of the Kharia,
Ho, and Munda poetry that he later published in 1942–43, as well
as the Bhojpuri songs that form the subject of this book. He had
hoped to write a scholarly census report on the model of those of Sir
Edward Gait and Walter G. Lacey, but wartime constraints made
this impossible. The statistics were published and the ethnographic
material had to be omitted. During this period Archer formed a
friendship with the anthropologist Verrier Elwin, who lived among
the Gonds of Central India and shared his interest in folk poetry.
Songs of the Forest: The Folk Poetry of the Gonds,[3] by Elwin and Shamrao
Hivale, was known to Archer when he wrote *The Blue Grove*. Archer
and Elwin took over joint editorship of the anthropological journal
Man in India after the death of Sarat Chandra Roy in 1942 and they
continued to edit it together until 1948. The journal served as a
vehicle for the publication of much village poetry and tribal literature
collected by them.

The most personally rewarding period in India for Archer was when
he served as Deputy Commissioner of the Santal Parganas in Dumka,
from 1942 to 1946. He had earlier become interested in the small
settlements of Santal tribals in the eastern part of the Purnea district. He was now able to extend his enquiries. His commitment to
the preservation of Santal culture involved him in a project to codify
Santal civil law so that it could be properly applied in the government
courts. Although, to Archer's profound disappointment, the report
was ignored after Independence, it served to document the integrity
of Santal culture. He also collected Santal songs, stories, and riddles,
as well as the scroll paintings made by the Jadupatua caste of min-
strels, who used them to illustrate the folk epics they recited for
Santal audiences. His book *The Hill of Flutes: Life, Love and Poetry
in Tribal India,* based on his studies and experiences, was published
in 1974.

Archer's posting to Patna as Collector in 1941, after the completion of the census, became the source of a completely new scholarly

adventure for him. In comparison with the exhilarating exoticism of rural Bihar, he at first found Patna as physically and spiritually dull as E. M. Forster had depicted it, under the place-name Chandra-pore, in A *Passage to India*. Archer alludes to this in his introduction to *Visions of Courtly India: The Archer Collection of Pahari Miniatures*, where he describes the circumstances under which he and Mildred began collecting Indian miniature paintings.

The Archers abhorred the formalities of British social life and were relieved that their quarters were near Patna University, where they found a more congenial society. In the Patna Museum, they began to learn about classical Indian sculpture, and through a friendship with the eminent barrister and art collector P. C. Manuk, they learned to appreciate miniature painting. At first Archer's aesthetic prefer-ence for modern and primitive art made him dismiss the exquisite figurative art of the miniatures, but his romantic core quickly suc-cumbed to the delicate intricacies of Punjab Hill painting. He notes, "It was as if I had stumbled on a collection of Elizabethan lyrics and was discovering for the first time the mainstream of English love-poetry. The language might not be modern. . . . but it expressed with matchless elegance the tender nuances of romantic passion. Manuk's Pahari pictures were the exact equivalents in Indian paint-ing of this English love-poetry."

With Manuk's help, the Archers began to collect paintings, and as collectors they developed friendships with other connoisseurs, in-cluding Rai Krishna Das, Gopi Krishna Kanoria, Moti Chandra, and Karl Khandalavala. This involvement with the visual art of princely India and with the circle of Indian collectors who studied it later proved essential to his scholarship on Indian painting and to his cur-atorial work at the Victoria and Albert Museum. Although the ethos of the feudal Hindu courts was vastly different from that of the folk and tribal cultures he had studied before, Archer approached this material with the same poetic passion and systematic attention to details of local geography, history, custom, and religious ritual that distinguished his anthropological work.

In reading his monumental two-volume work *Indian Paintings from the Punjab Hills,* one feels that the author's reconstruction of the personality of each ruler through portraits, travelers' records, and state documents gave him an intimate grasp of the courtly context of the paintings, parallel to the social contexts within which he studied folk and tribal art forms. By carefully observing the interaction between traditions of painting and influences of patronage, he was able to identify distinctive types of local painting within a period of three centuries in the Punjab hills. His evocative descriptions of individual paintings draw on the poetry of Sanskrit and vernacular traditions to penetrate the symbolic richness of each picture.

It was during his field work as Census Superintendent from 1939 to 1940 that Archer was able to gather varied evidence of the creative life of the village women of Bihar, as expressed in their visual art, singing, and ritual performances. Clues to this had come in earlier discoveries. When he was in Madhubani during the earthquake of 1934, he had not only seen the brilliant murals on cracked walls, but had also learned that the women who painted them preserved an oral tradition of singing the erotic lyrics of the Maithili poet Vidyāpati. He had begun a collection and study of these, which was eventually published in collaboration with Deben Bhattacharya as *Love Songs of Vidyāpati.* When he returned to study the work of the women painters of Mithila, he realized that the paintings functioned as an integral part of village life and were inextricably related to the various religious rituals which the women controlled. They were especially important in marriage ceremonies.[4]

From ancient times, marriage has been the most auspicious celebration in Hindu religious life.[5] In every part of North India it remains not only the focal economic and social event for the Hindu family, but an auspicious occasion that calls into play the imaginative and artistic resources of the village world. Participation of various village castes is a notable part of the wedding rituals. In Bihar, in addition to the Brahman priest, performers may include the barber

and his wife, the washerman, the Chamar, a leatherworker who plays
the ritual drum, and the Bari, the traditional maker of leaf plates
and cups for festivals, who acts as a messenger.

The basic form of wedding that Archer observed in Bihar traditionally begins with a series of rituals that culminate a month or
more later in the actual marriage (biwāh, or vivāh). This is followed
by "second marriage" (gaunā), which marks the bride's move to her
husband's household. The second marriage may take place from one
to seven years after the first, depending on the age of the girl. When
the bride and groom are mature, as is often the case among highly
educated Kayasths and Brahmans, first and second marriage rituals
would blend in the wedding.

In Mithila, when a wedding is to take place, the women artists of
the village immediately start their work. The women paint the courtyard walls of the houses of the bride and groom with images of protective and exemplary deities, which vary according to season, wedding-
date, caste, family, and astrological predictions. Mildred Archer
summarizes their purpose, as it was explained to her more than forty
years ago:

It was essential to associate all the main gods and goddesses with the event
so that they might shower blessings. Radha and Krishna, Shiva and Parvati,
Vishnu and Lakshmi, Ganesha, Rama and Sita, Durga, Kali, and the Jagan-
natha trio all made their appearance. Frequently the bride and bridegroom
with their attendants were also depicted so that they might appear to be
participating in the scene and thus be associated with these auspicious beings.
Equally important were designs incorporating a number of propitious symbols: a ring of lotuses, flowers, a 'bamboo tree,' parrots, turtles, fishes, the
sun and moon, flowering trees, and elephants.[6]

The most elaborate murals are reserved for the kohbar, the marriage chamber in which the bride and groom spend their first nights
together. This room is painted by a female relative of the bride or
groom at their respective houses. The lotus ring and the bamboo tree
figure most prominently as fertility imagery because of their rapid

growth and visual analogy to sexual organs. The paintings are never purely decorative, but serve to form a vibrant symbolic stage for the rituals.

The older women of the household are usually responsible for the main designs and the younger women and girls fill in the details and colors. Many households have for generations kept records of the family's traditional designs, executed on paper in pen-and-ink and sometimes with watercolors, as aides-mémoire. The young bride would take these to her new home and in this way the old motifs were transmitted to the next generation. Wall painting is not exclusive to Mithila, but nowhere else in Bihar has it been practiced with such intensity and strength of design.

The rich symbolism of the Kayasth paintings in Mithila relates closely to the images used by the Kayasth women of Shahabad in their songs. Mildred and I have therefore chosen to illustrate the songs with a few examples of aides-mémoire and photographs collected from Kayasth households in Mithila in 1938 and 1940. No such paintings are known from Shahabad, nor is there evidence that an elaborate tradition of women's painting ever existed there. The paintings referred to in the Bhojpuri songs are simple diagrams and designs painted in the marriage chamber.

In each area, distinctive songs are also a vital part of marriage festivals and young girls learn these from their mothers, grandmothers, and aunts. On every day of the extended marriage period, local women and the families of both the bride and groom assemble in their respective houses every morning and evening to sing wedding songs. Like the paintings, the songs are perceived to enhance the auspiciousness of the rituals, ward off evil influences, and assure the success of the marriage. Like much of the ritual, the songs are also didactic, serving to impress both bride and groom with the reality of their social and sexual union.

As the locus for his detailed study of the marriage rituals, Archer chose households of the Srivastav subcaste of the Kayasth caste[7] living within a small area of the Bhojpuri-speaking[8] region of Shahabad district, where he had first been posted in 1931, Shahabad (now Arrah district) is southwest of Mithila, on the other side of the Ganges, and its ceremonial life is distinct in many ways from that of Mithila. Within the Bhojpuri Kayasth community, women valued the preservation and performance of songs far more than the art of painting and they seemed proud of their oral tradition.[9] Some families kept notebooks of songs and these were also used in the collection process. During the course of the census operations, one of Archer's Kayasth assistants, Babu Sankta Prasad, helped him with the work of collecting, analyzing, and translating the rituals and songs. This collaboration is remarkable since few European or Indian men at that time considered the songs, rituals, and stories of women appropriate objects of study and few could have penetrated the separateness of the women's world with such sensitivity.

Recent studies of marriage songs and rituals in the Bhojpuri area show that the traditions Archer recorded about forty years ago are alive today, not only in Kayasth households, but in high-caste communities throughout the region. Variations are due to time, location, and subcaste, as well as to the eye of each observer. Though the communities differ and the songs and practices have evolved in time, the forms Archer describes remain relevant to understanding the way in which the Bhojpuri women conceive their world.[10]

Although all of the songs are sung by the women of the wedding households and their relatives, the songs have many voices, often delineated in lyric dialogues. The dramatis personae include the bride, her mother, her brother's wife and her sisters, the groom's mother and the groom. The bride does not actually sing the songs, but the dominant voice is hers. For the bride, marriage means a separation from the world of childhood and the songs are filled with sadness and even anger. Her frightening new role as a subordinate woman in a strange household is often either explicit or implied, even when she is not the subject of the song. Through such songs the women express their collective feelings, attitudes, and beliefs. The young bride is made acutely aware of the difficulties she will face in the awkward transition to her new status by this ritualized display of shared emotions.[11]

In addition to the obvious interest of the songs themselves, the value of Archer's study lies in his ethnographic focus and in his meticulous attention to the objects, gestures, sounds, and colors which constitute the rituals in which the songs are embedded. What is lacking is an analysis of the musical forms of the songs, but this was outside Archer's interest and competence.[12] Though he had no special anthropological training or concern with rival theories of social structure, Archer fully recognized the role of the songs and rituals in effecting a social transformation.[13] His insistence on providing the social and ritual context for the songs and his sensitivity to the interpretive categories of the participants make the work an important document. Its unrelenting detail and recording of intricate sequences, somewhat like a choreographer's notation for every movement of a ballet, reveals the rituals and songs as elements of a complex symbolic process, one that does not lend itself to easy summary.

New York   BARBARA STOLER MILLER
July 1984

1. Design of lotus circles *(kamalban)*. Seven lotus circles pierced by a bamboo tree surrounded by parrots. By a Maithil Kayasth woman from the household of Markanda Jha, village Basauli, Madhubani, Darbhanga district, Bihar, c. 1920–40. Colored ink. Presented to W. G. Archer, 1940.

2. Veiled bride with parrot and flowers. By a Maithil Kayasth woman from the household of Sabhapati Das, village Darema, Darbhanga, Darbhanga district, Bihar, c. 1920–40. Pen-and-ink and watercolor. Presented to W. G. Archer by the household, 1940.

3. Lakshmī lustrated by elephants and Gangā on a fantastic crocodile (*makara*). Mural from the bridal chamber at the house of Mohan Lal Das, village Darema, Darbhanga, Darbhanga district, Bihar. 1940.

4. Shiva riding on his bull, with Pārvatī; and Shiva alone. Mural from the bridal chamber of the house of Mohan Lal Das, village Darema, Darbhanga, Dharbhanga district, Bihar. 1940.

5. Hanumān with three monkeys. Marriage mural from the veranda of the house of Ram Krishna Das, village Baujparaul, Nauratan tola, Benipatti, Darbhanga district. 1940. Red, black, and yellow.

6. Bridesmaids carrying the elephant and the plate. Behind them, part of a kadam tree with Krishna partly visible at the top; peacocks in the tree and a swing suspended from its branches; on the swing, a child, perhaps the infant Krishna being swung by two girls; on the right a figure with a lantern. Mural from the bridal chamber of the house of Ram Adin Das, village Keoti, Darbhanga, Darbhanga district. 1940. Red and black.

7. Veiled brides below a bullock. Mural from the veranda of the
house of Ram Krishna Das, village Baujparaul, Benipati, Darbhanga
district. 1940. Pink, mauve, yellow.

8. Camels surrounded by plants and flowers. Mural in the outer veranda of the house of Kirtipati Das, village Darema, Darbhanga, Darbhanga district. 1940.

9. Two women surrounded with flowers. Murals in an inner room of the house of Suriabansi Das, village Samaila, Darbhanga, Darbhanga district. 1936. Red and black.

10. Durgā on a lion killing a demon, and Ganesh with rats. Mural in the bridal chamber of the house of Gokul Bihari Das, village Bachhi, Madhubani, Darbhanga district. 1940. Yellow, blue and pink.

11. Tortoise and boar incarnations of Vishnu. Mural from the bridal chamber of the house of Mohan Lal Das, village Darema, Darbhanga, Darbhanga district. 1940. Dull red and black.

12. Painted clay marriage plate showing Krishna and two milkmaids with cowherds, apsaras, and flowers. Made at the house of Mohan Lal Das, village Darema, Darbhanga, Darbhanga district. 1940.

13. Auspicious clay elephant. In the background, lotus and bamboo tree design. In the bridal chamber of the house of Sitanath Jha, Village Ujan, Bahera, Sadr subdivision, Darbhanga district. 1940.

BIBLIOGRAPHY OF THE WRITINGS OF

WILLIAM G. ARCHER

I. WORKS BY W. G. ARCHER

The Blue Grove: The Poetry of the Uraons. London: Allen & Unwin, 1940.

The Vertical Man: A Study in Primitive Indian Sculpture. London: Allen and Unwin, 1947.

The Plains of the Sun. London: Routledge, 1948.

The Dove and the Leopard: More Uraon Poetry. Calcutta: Orient Longmans, 1948.

Indian Painting in the Punjab Hills. London: H.M.S.O., 1952.

Kangra Painting. London: Faber & Faber, 1952. Second and revised impression, 1953.

Bazaar Paintings of Calcutta. London: H.M.S.O., 1953.

Garhwal Painting. London: Faber & Faber, 1954. Second and revised impression, 1955.

Indian Painting. London: Batsford, 1956.

The Loves of Krishna. London: Allen & Unwin, 1957.

Indian Paintings from Rajasthan. London: Arts Council of Great Britain, 1957.

Central Indian Painting. London: Faber & Faber, 1957.

India and Modern Art. London: Allen & Unwin, 1959.

Indian Painting in Bundi and Kotah. London: H.M.S.O., 1959.

Indian Miniatures. London, New York: Studio Books, 1960.

Kalighat Drawings. Bombay: Marg Publications, 1962.

Paintings of the Sikhs. London: H.M.S.O., 1966.

Kalighat Paintings. London: H.M.S.O., 1971.

Indian Paintings from the Punjab Hills, 2 vols. London: Sotheby Parke Bernet, 1973.

The Hill of Flutes: Life, Love and Poetry in Tribal India. London: Allen & Unwin, 1974.

Tribal Law and Justice: A Report on the Santal. New Delhi: Concept Press, 1984.

II. CO-AUTHORED BY W. G. ARCHER AND:

Robert Melville. *Forty Thousand Years of Modern Art.* London: Institute of Contemporary Art, 1948.

Mildred Archer. *Indian Painting for the British.* Oxford: Oxford University Press, 1955.

S. Paranavitana. *Ceylon: Paintings from Temple, Shrine, and Rock.* New York: Unesco World Art Series, 1957.

D. Bhattacharya. *Love Songs of Vidyapati.* London: Allen & Unwin, 1963.

Edwin Binney, 3rd. *Rajput Miniatures.* Portland, Oregon: Portland Art Museum, 1968.

S. Paranavitana. *"The Sigiri Grafitti": An Anthology of Sinhalese Literature,* ed. C. Reynolds. London: Allen & Unwin, 1970.

III. PREFACES AND FOREWORDS BY W. G. ARCHER TO:

Verrier Elwin. *Folk Songs of Chhattisgarh.* London: Oxfird University Press, 1946.

M. S. Randhawa. *Kangra Valley Painting.* New Delhi: Government of India, 1954.

M. S. Randhawa. *Kangra Paintings of the Gita Govinda.* New Delhi: National Museum, 1963.

The Kama Sutra. Translated by Sir Richard Burton and F. F. Arbuthnot. London: Allen & Unwin, 1963.

The Gulistan of Sadi. Translated by Edward Rehatsek. London: Allen & Unwin, 1964.

The Koka Shastra. Translated with an introduction and notes by Alex
  Comfort. London: Allen & Unwin, 1964.

IV. ARTICLES

"Maithil Painting." *Marg* (1949), 3(3):24–33.
"Some Nurpur Paintings." *Marg* (1955), 8(3):8–18.
"Problems of Painting in the Punjab Hills." *Marg* (1957), 10(2):30–36.
"Survey of Rajasthani Styles: Kotah." *Marg* (1958), 11(2):65–67.

V. INDIAN ETHNOLOGY: Contributions to *Man in India*
(Ranchi) During Period of Joint Editorship with Verrier Elwin,
1942–48

"Seasonal Songs of Patna District" (1942), 22:233–37.
"A Short Anthology of Indian Folk Poetry: Comment" (1943), 23:1–3.
"Baiga Poetry" (1943), 23:47–60.
"Santal Poetry" (1943), 23:98–105.
"An Anthology of Indian Marriage Sermons" (1943), 23:106–10.
"Betrothal Dialogues" (1943), 23:147–53.
"Murder in Tribal India: Comment" (1943), 23:179–81.
"An Indian Riddle Book" (1943), 23:265–315.
"Extracts from a Riddle Notebook" (1943), 23:323–41.
"Festival Songs" (1944), 24:70–74.
"Diwali Painting" (1944), 24:82–84.
"More Santal Songs" (1944), 24:141–44.
"The Illegitimate Child in Santal Society" (1944), 24:154–69.
"Folk-tales in Tribal India" (1944), 24:207–9.
"The Forcible Marriage" (1945), 25:29–42.
"Rebellions in Tribal India" (1945), 25:205–6.
"Santal Rebellion Songs" (1945), 25:207.
"The Santal Rebellion" (1945), 25:223–39.
"Santal Transplantation Songs" (1946), 26:6–7.
"Sabai Cultivation in the Rajmahal Hills" (1946), 26:12–19.
"Tribal Administration: Comment" (1946), 26:79–80.

"Tribal Justice: Comment" (1946), 26:151–53.
"Two Kharia Weddings" (1946), 26:215–19.
"Ritual Friendship in Santal Society" (1947), 27:57–60.
"The Santal Treatment of Witchcraft" (1947), 27:103–21.

VI. TRIBAL TEXTS: Collections of Indian Village and Tribal
Poetry in the Vernacular, by W. G. Archer and:

F. Hahn and Dharamdas Lakra. *Lil Khora Khekhel:* A Collection of
2,600 Uraon Songs and 440 Riddles in Uraon and Gaonwari.
Laheriasarai, 1941.

B. K. Dutt and Ram Chandra Birua. *Ho Durang:* A Collection of 935
Ho Songs and 400 Riddles in Ho. Patna, 1942.

Jatru Kharia, Daud Dungdung, and Manmaeeh Totetohran. *Kharia
Along:* A Collection of 1,528 Kharia Songs and 446 Riddles in
Kharia. Ranchi, 1942.

Dilbar Hans and Samuel Hans. *Munda Durang:* A Collection of 1,641
Munda Songs and 380 Riddles in Mundari. Patna, 1942.

Gopal Gamaliel Soren. *Hor Seren:* A Collection of 1,676 Santal Songs
in Santali. Dumka, 1943.

Gopal Gamaliel Soren. *Don Soren:* A Collection of 1,954 Santal Cultivation and Marriage Songs in Santali. Dumka, 1943.

Stephan H. Murmu. *Hor Kudum:* A Collection of 492 Santal Riddles
in Santali. Dumka, 1944.

AUTHOR'S PREFACE

In the Indian province of Bihar, village poetry falls into two groups. The first consists of the poetry of the aboriginal tribes—a poetry which is chiefly confined to Chota Nagpur and the Santal Parganas and includes the songs of Santals, Uraons, Mundas, Hos, and Kharias.[1] These songs are village poetry in the sense that the village as a whole produces them. They are sung at weddings and dances in which the greater part of the village joins. They are not the prerogative of one sex only, for boys and men sing them equally with girls and women. They are almost always linked to dancing and are thus a form of dance poetry. They are sung as part of a whole public scene which men and women irrespective of their families can come and witness. Finally in a special sense the poetry is the property of the tribe that sings it. There is not a single tribal poetry common to Santals, Uraons, Hos, and Mundas. There is rather a series of tribal poetries—each expressing the culture of a tribe.

The second group of poetry, on the other hand, covers the village songs of Hindu castes and contains a wide variety of types. Ahir men, for example, sing a number of grazing songs, which range from the short *biraha* to the long *chanchar* while Mushahars, Dusadhs, and Doms have legends which the men sing at night. Such poetry is essentially male and is the distinctive product of each caste. Almost all other Hindu village poetry, on the other hand, is hardly ever masculine but is composed and sung by the women. It is village poetry in the sense that the village makes it and it is scarcely ever the work of a single author. It is hardly ever sung in public and though the conditions of privacy are never quite complete, men and strangers are virtually excluded. It is sometimes sung as entertainment and occasionally used in love-making but in other respects it is always used as an adjunct to ritual. Moreover it is never linked to dancing and is largely religious. Lastly, although each of the major Hindu castes has its own reserve of village poetry, there is no caste poetry in the sense in which there is a poetry of a tribe. The songs sung by the upper castes overlap continually. They draw on the same mythology, the same ritual, the same verse forms, the same social background. Hindu village poetry is a caste selection of the poetry of an area, a caste anthology rather than a purely caste product.

In this book, I have illustrated this second type of village poetry— the poetry of the Hindu Kayasth caste. With the exception of a few songs recorded in Patna, the poems were collected from Kayasth households in the Bihar district of Shahabad and the language of most of the originals is Bhojpuri, a dialect of Bihari Hindi. This dialect has been called "a handy article made for current use, not too much encumbered by grammatical subtleties and suitable to an alert active people."[2] It is characterized by its long drawled vowels, its fondness for labials, and its musical rhythms. An English which favored words like "candle," "dangle," "ladle," and "meddle" would be an appropriate analogy. These Bhojpuri originals I have published partly in the *Journal of the Bihar Research Society* (1942, 1943) and more fully in *Bhojpūrī Grām Gīt* (Patna, 1943).

All these poems could be claimed as defining, within certain limits, Kayasth village culture. But they are also representative of Brahman, Bhumihar Brahman, and Rajput village poetry not only in Shahabad but elsewhere, and in this connection the songs may be compared with the originals in *Kabita Kaumudī, Part 5, Grām Gīt*.[3] These latter poems were collected from the Saran and Champaran districts of North Bihar and from the Eastern districts of the United Provinces. Their caste origin is not recorded but it is obvious that both collections spring from a single regional culture. This culture is in part the culture of Bhojpur—an area which overlaps into the districts of Gorakhpur and Ballia in the United Provinces and in language includes much of Patna and Saran in Bihar. But it is also the culture of a much wider area and in fact the poems are not untypical of upper-caste village poetry in the whole Hindi-speaking area of Eastern India.

Since the poems are often adjuncts to ritual, I have added accounts both of the wedding ceremonies and the rites of birth. The ritual is of great importance, for not only does it provide the social setting for many of the poems but it is itself a projection of poetic methods. The actions which comprise the ritual are prompted by the same ways of thought and feeling as those which underlie the poetry. The ritual is a social occasion for poetry and at the same time a form of poetry itself.

It is for this reason that I have attempted an interpretation of the wedding rites and in so doing have used a method defended by Wilhelm Worringer in *Form in Gothic*.[4] For, apart from comparison and intuition, no other method is possible. The essence of the ritual is that much of its symbolism should be latent. If it were completely conscious, it would lose its mystery, and in its mystery lies its power. Yet the mystery is only a guise for a basic meaning. To make no attempt to expose that meaning would be to treat it as an idle show, boring and without compulsion. Such a treatment would merely mislead, and at the risk of erring in detail I have ventured to treat the wedding ceremony as what in essence it is—a work of art. It is as part of this enveloping work of art that the poems should be read.

With the exception of the *dohās*, which may also be composed by males, all the poems are sung only by women. While a few may have been composed by individuals, all of them are now regarded as anonymous and traditional. Communal singing favors this kind of transmission. It is noteworthy that many Kayasth households keep family copybooks. In these books the ancestral songs are written down and the books act as aides-mémoire, which maintain the tradition.

The poems are never actually sung nor are they intended to be sung outside their ritual context. Their object is to enhance a ritual situation and the situation itself is by implication a part of each poem.

In many of the poems, the wedding situation is magnified by comparison with Hindu mythological figures, such as Rām and Sītā or Shiva
and Gaurī.[5] The poem gives the bride and bridegroom a religious
background and thus imbues the occasion with grandeur. At the same
time, the chanting of divine names, and their injection into the wedding, gives it an auspicious aura. The sense of magnificence may also
be qualified by humor. Shiva poems, for example, often combine the
glory of Shiva's wedding with the plight of Gaurī. When sung at
weddings, they magnify and at the same time deflate the bridal pair.
Such a sense of joking is part of the relaxed atmosphere of a wedding. In yet other poems, such as the ornamentation songs (sehalā),
all the accoutrements of a bride and bridegroom are described as if
they had an ideal beauty. Every bride is as lovely as a princess and
every bridegroom is a rājā, or king, for two and a half days. The
value of the songs is that they effect a social transformation.

To the many who assisted me at various stages of this book, I am
deeply grateful—particularly to Dr. A. P. Banerjee-Sastri and the
Council of the Bihar Research Society for valuable help in publishing
the originals; to Mr. B. B. Mukharji and Mr. Hiralal Jalan, but for
whose interest Bhojpūrī Grām Gīt might never have been printed; to
Dr. Verrier Elwin and Mr. Sadashiva Prasad for constant advice and
criticism; to Mr. N. C. Bhattacherjee, who supplied me with a map;
and to Mildred Archer for constant stimulus and advice. Above all,
my special thanks are due to Babu Sankta Prasad. Himself a Kayasth,
he was tireless in giving me information about Kayasth life and manners while for translation his alert intelligence was always at my
service to explain dialect words and elucidate meanings.

Versions of certain songs have appeared in Man in India and in
The Wind and the Rain, and to the editors of these journals I make
the fullest acknowledgment.

April 1944   W. G. ARCHER

THE MARRIAGE RITUAL

THE RITUAL SYMBOLS

How do we profess to arrive at the meaning of these dream-symbols, about which the dreamer himself can give us little or no information?

My answer is that we derive our knowledge from widely different sources: from fairy tales and myths, jokes and witticisms, from folklore, i.e. from what we know of the manners and customs, sayings and songs, of different peoples, and from poetic and colloquial usage of language. Everywhere in these various fields the same symbolism occurs, and in many of them we can understand it without being taught individually, we shall find so many parallels to dream-symbolism that we are bound to be convinced of the correctness of our interpretations —Freud, *Introductory Lectures on Psycho-analysis.*

It is only at the approach of the fantastic at a point where human reason loses its control that the most profound emotion of the individual has the fullest opportunity to express itself: emotion unsuitable for projection in the frame-work of the real world and which has no other solution in its urgency than to rely on the eternal solicitation of symbols and myths —Andre Breton, *What is Surrealism?*[1]

I

If we are to find an analogy for this wedding ritual, the nearest would be a surrealist poem, ballet, or novel. In a surrealist work the action has a strange power and a mysterious charm. Strange persons develop their intriguing contacts and the action has an air of irrational urgency. On analysis it is seen that many of the actions are symbolic and the poem, novel, or ballet generates its power from the semi-conscious associations which its dialogue, gestures, scenery, and action evoke.[2] In the ritual of a Kayasth wedding, there is a similar use of irrational action, a similar use of persons with a strangely inflated power, and a similar use of semiconscious symbols. The meaning of the ritual may be submerged and, for many, may be scarcely comprehended but its basis is in a symbolic system and its total effect is overpowering.

The meaning of the ritual may be interpreted as follows. The wedding is a passage from one state of life to another. The boy and girl shed their former states, enter a sanctified period in which their virginity is intensified, and finally reach a new state in which they are united. The object of their union is to enhance their vitality—to place their lives on an adult basis—and, as a corollary, to produce children. It is a passage from a state of virginity to a state of fertility. As a result of the union of persons, the two families are also united and the boy and the girl come together not simply as individuals but as members of their families. The action not only transforms two persons but it puts two groups into a new and vital relation with each other.

If we now examine the ritual from this point of view, much that is at first bewildering and obscure takes on the most lucid significance. The girl starts her passage when she is rubbed with turmeric paste (haldī) on the day of the first auspicious rites (sāgun) and is given an old white sari. For ten days she does not wash and wears the same sari. This break with her daily routine ushers her into the new state. Then on the day of anointment, five to three days before the wedding, she is smeared all over with haldī, made entirely "aseptic,"[3] and is put in the nuptial chamber (kohbar). The days that follow are neither a blank nor a jump, for on each day the ritual smearing is again performed. Each day moves her further on the passage and intensifies her virgin state. Finally, on the wedding night, she is washed in a virgin trench, her body is again rubbed with paste and then rinsed with water, and finally the sullied water of the bridegroom is poured over her. With this contact with the bridegroom she starts to leave her former state until finally the journey with her husband takes her out of it and she merges into his family.

While the girl is moving on her passage, the boy is also following a parallel and similar course. On his day of anointment he is smeared with turmeric paste and from then on until the wedding, he is segregated and his "aseptic" state continued with daily smearings.

During this period, and until the wedding is over, sympathetic action is taken to intensify the virgin state. Freshly dug earth is brought for making the wedding hearth. Green bamboos and fresh mango leaves are used for the wedding canopy. New pitchers are used throughout the course of the wedding. Fresh turmeric is crushed into a paste at the *haldī* ceremony; and the boy and girl squat over newly made trenches and are washed in fresh water.

Side by side with this positive action, negative steps are also taken. Evil spirits are banished and evil eyes are averted. At each stage, blessing gestures are performed. If the boy and girl have to leave their rooms at night, they are accompanied by companions to shield them from marauding spirits. And finally, on the wedding day, the girl is particularly protected from the evil eye and from evil spirits by the encircling of her head with mustard. In this way the virginity of the bride and bridegroom is both enhanced and preserved.

Up to the wedding day the ritual aims at intensifying the virginity of the boy and girl, but with the approach of the wedding day itself two new factors enter. The boy and girl are severed from their former lives, their union is accomplished and they enter the new state.

This severence is demonstrated in the following ways. The virgin period is first brought to a close through the feast of the five virgins and the five bachelors. A pantomime of severence is then performed. The mother cuts the boy's nail. The boy bites the mango stalks and spits them in his mother's hand and finally his mother pours water into his mouth and he spits it out. The cutting, the biting, and the spitting are all images of severence and rejection. Similarly with the girl, the nail of the little finger is cut and the five mango leaves are bitten, and when she starts for her husband's home after the wedding she is given water to spit from her mouth. In all these ways the bride and bridegroom are severed from their former state.

But while this severence is being accomplished their union is also being shown, and for this, four methods are employed—the mutual exchange of articles, the sharing of food, the performance of common acts, and the linking of hands and clothes. Thus on the day of anointment the girl is rubbed with *haldī* in which *haldī* from the boy's house is mixed; and on the wedding day she is washed in water brought from the boy's house and in which the boy has been washed. The bridegroom dresses on the wedding day in a shawl presented by the girl's father at the time of the dowry. After the feast of the virgins, the bridegroom eats a nut which his wife has sucked. In the wedding shed, the bride sits on her father's lap, the bridegroom's hands are placed on top of hers, and her brother pours water on the linked hands. The bride and bridegroom hold hands while they make the marriage declarations. They go round the shed seven times together. The boy's shawl is tied to the girl's sari and a nut, a copper coin, and rice are knotted in it. Rice is thrown over them together. In the bridal chamber, the bride eats some curds and sugar and the bridegroom eats what is left. Before leaving for the bridegroom's house, the girl goes with the boy into the chamber. He stands behind her, puts his arms through her armpits, and holds her hands—rice is sprinkled on him and he tosses it over his back five times.

Finally the girl is absorbed into the boy's family. The journey in the litter and the bridge of baskets ensure that nothing will impair her new state. Her introduction to the fundamentals of the household and the contents of the kitchen and storeroom identifies her with the household; and finally the leaf waistlet which protected her throughout her passage but which might now impede consummation is finally removed. Nothing is now left. The passage is over. The new state is reached and the scene closes on the bridegroom's bed.

II

To reduce the structure of this ritual is to emphasize its basic meaning; but its total impact will not be understood unless certain other elements are explained—elements which are omnipresent and which charge it with mystery and power.

The most important of these is a sexual or fertility element which takes, in all, four forms.

The first may be summarized as a general release of sexual jokes. The flower girl, for example, when she comes with the bridegroom's crown, is treated as if she were his mistress. The drummer who beats the drum when the mother goes for the earth-digging ceremony is hailed as her paramour. It is taken for granted that the maidservant who travels with the bridegroom on his way to the bride's house is far from innocent. The five girl bearers of the Kahar caste who carry the food wrapped in scarlet paper to the boy's party are greeted in sexual terms. At the door of the bridal chamber the bridegroom is required to make some sexual offers. If the absence of his mother is excused, he has to offer a sister for the sexual amusement of the bride's brother. Throughout the songs there is a tendency to attribute laxity both to the boy and to his parents. He is the little bastard, the son of a loose woman. Finally at the wedding dinner the boy's father is twitted as if he had gone to bed with the girl's mother. In these sexual jokes is a release of repressed energy which when applied to the marriage must necessarily make it fertile.

Secondly there is the use of symbols for the sexual act. The most obvious is the insertion of the rice pounder in the mortar after the earth digging ceremony. This is accompanied by a song which stresses its sexual character and leaves no doubt of its function as a sexual diagram.[4] But besides this act there are others in which the symbolism is present, if less clearly exposed. Thus, at the earth digging ceremony, the knocking of the five betel leaves and the rice into the mother's lap, as well as the pouring of water in a single jet by the well, are symbols of the sexual act.[5] Again, when the wedding canopy is being erected, the bride's forearms are measured and the central square is marked out in terms of their length. In the center of this private square, a hole is dug and into it a bamboo shaft is formally set down.[6] Similarly on the day of anointment the girl's hand is filled with rice and a bangle is squeezed over it, while the piercing of a newly made toy ram is also a diagram of what the wedding will require from the bridegroom. The effect of these diagrams on the ritual is, as it were, to insert a set of electrical charges. Linked with the sexual joking, they create an atmosphere in which virginity blends with all that is adult and fertile.

A third way in which the fertility of the wedding is promoted is by the engagement of dancing-girls. As the evening fades, the dancing-girl stands, sings her songs, and pirouettes before the guests. She jingles the dancing bells on her ankles, stamping in time to a tabor. She goes round in little circles stiffly oscillating as she goes, and every now and then setting up a circular roll of her buttocks. Within this narrow range of gestures, her dancing is mechanically set and the bridegroom's party passes the darker hours of the night by watching this. It is true that the ostensible reason for her presence is entertainment but it is impossible to purge her completely of all sexual functions. She provides, as it were, an overtone of sexuality. She acts as a target for wishes. She hints at the wilder joys of romance. Above all, the nature of her trade makes her particularly auspicious for the bride. Since she is always by implication a prostitute, she can never be married and therefore can never be a widow. Accordingly her presence opens up for the bride a vista of long and happy wifehood. The dancing girl is a talisman by which the bride's life-long status is assured.

Finally, throughout the ritual, two groups of "disguised" fertility objects play their part. The first consists of ingredients in the worship—such as rice, paddy, betel, nuts, vermilion powder *(sindūr)*, sacred grasses, and mango leaves. All of these are conventionally holy and are doubtless used in part for this reason. But behind their conventional use in worship lies a wider symbolism and it is in fact to this symbolism that we must look to explain their original selection. *Sindūr* and the evergreen mango, for example, are symbols of vitality—the *sindūr* with its vermilion color pointing to blood, while the evergreen leaves are symbols of long life. *Dūb, kush,* and *munj* grass,[7] with their prolific growth, share with all grass a certain fertility relevance while their fine texture makes them the most suitable forms for use in worship. Rice is a staple form of food and a natural image of fertility[8] while nuts are almost universally associated with pregnancy.[9] When the bride and bridegroom handle nuts, are marked with scarlet powder, or are sprinkled with rice, the ritual is fulfilling a dual function. On one level it is sanctifying but on another it is fertilizing.

The second group consists of objects which are mainly scenic, which act as passive witnesses but which by their motionless presence charge the action with import. They include the bowerlike wedding canopy, the earthen hearth and the mud platform, the curry-stone,[10] the plough shaft, the green bamboo stick and the green mango leaves, the plantain posts, and finally the bridal pitcher.

Of these, the wedding canopy is at first appearance merely a utility structure made of green bamboos and decorated with mango leaves. But the materials are significant, for through their prolific character the bamboos symbolize fertility while their swaying lines afford a sexual overtone. Similarly the mango points to fertility for its fruit is a common image for the breasts. With its bamboo and mango leaves, the canopy creates, as it were, all the conditions which are necessary for having children.

The earthen hearth and the mud platform. The earthen hearth is made from virgin earth dug out by women on the outskirts of the village in the *matkorā* ceremony. The mud platform in the middle of the marriage bower is made from fresh mud taken from near a well. In the first of these the earth is introduced as a witness—the more powerful because it is the source of life; while in the second, it has the added force of a sexual allegory. The earth with its passive horizontal qualities is fertilized by the vertical jet of water; and it is as married earth that it occupies its central place.

The curry-stone and roller, the plough shaft, the green bamboo stick, and the green mango leaves. These are put under the wedding canopy on the day of anointment. The bamboo stick and the mango leaves fulfil a fertility function while the plough shaft is a mixed economic and sexual image—a sign of the toil without which the staple food of the family cannot be obtained, but also a disguised reference to the sexual act.[11] The curry-stone and roller are respectively the female and the male.[12]

The plantain posts. These are put up partly for decoration—their large feathery leaves affording a graceful contrast to the brick or mud walls of the house, but also because the plantain with its prolific and phallic fruit is a symbol of fertility.[13]

The bridal pitcher. This is the most important of all the "scenic" objects, for in its composition it includes all the basic symbols. As a pitcher of water it symbolizes the womb, while the copper coin and nut which are dropped into it represent its fertilization. The paddy which is heaped on its lid and the mango leaves placed on its rims are symbols of the fecund results which should attend the wedding. But it is not only as a diagram of fecundity that it has its power, for its union of rice and water—the fundamentals of life—makes it also the most solemn of witnesses. In accomplishing the rite of union in its presence the bride and bridegroom are not only blessed with fecundity but are warned of the gravity and mystery of their act. The bridal pitcher sums up all the irrational power of the ritual.

III

We have so far examined certain underlying motifs in the ritual. The rites would not however be powerful if their general effect were incoherent; there are three ways in which the parallel passages of the virgin and the bachelor are given form.

The first is through the symbolic use of the color red. At the engagement and dowry ceremonies, the boy is dressed in red and his brow is dabbed with vermilion. At the earth digging, red is put on the mattock and the drum. The mother's feet are reddened, vermilion is put on her forehead, and vermilion is put on the dug earth. At the second earth digging, vermilion marks are put on the well. Then again when the bridegroom's party is preparing the girl's presents, they wrap them in red paper and mark the baskets with vermilion.

A red sari, a red blouse, and a red skirt are included in the presents. On the wedding day the bridegroom wears red stockings, a red shirt, and a red turban. After his arrival in the girl's village five girl bearers of the Kahar caste bring him sweets wrapped in red cloth; in the wedding bower the bridegroom marks the bridal pot and the images of Gaurī and Ganesh with vermilion and puts vermilion on the girl's forehead five times when the girl leaves for her husband's house. She wears a red sari and sits on a red couch in the litter. She is marked with vermilion when she reaches his house. She again wears a red sari when the refuse of the marriage meal is disposed of in the boy's house.

This use of red almost certainly originated as a blood substitute but its function is now much wider. It pervades the passage with good luck and symbolizes all that is most vital while through its recurring presence it gives a unity to the action.

A similar function is performed by the number five. For the dowry ceremony, five envoys go. During the preliminary ceremonies the songs are sung in groups of five. The earth digging occurs five or eight days before the wedding. On the ceremonial diagram offerings are made in five places. Five small baskets are taken to the field. Five betel leaves are knocked from the drum five times. Five women lift the big basket onto the head of the barber's wife. The mother makes five cuts on the ground. Five women clasp the pounder and pound the rice. Five women sprinkle the earth with water. Five mango leaves are put in the mother's mouth and the boy bites them. Five bachelors dine together. When the bride's father goes to invite the party to his house five Kahar girls go with him carrying sweets. At the central wedding rite the bridegroom puts scarlet on the girl's brow five times. When the bride reaches the husband's house, she walks on five baskets and clasps five pots in the nuptial chamber.

The reason for this use of five is necessarily obscure, but perhaps as in China, where odd numbers are considered male and lucky and even numbers female and unlucky, similar ideas may possibly have determined Hindu selection. Abbott, in *The Keys of Power,* has stressed the energy (*shakti*) which attaches to this number. "The body," he says,

is made up of five elements and to avert the evil attaching to the body five things are necessarily offered in worship. The number five is also closely associated with the cross; the four points of an equal limbed cross and the centre make five and these determine the number of articles used in ritual. . . . The finality of five, its power to collect and gather energy from the directions makes it an almost indispensible number.[14]

Its function in the wedding ritual is plain. It gives unity to the most diverse elements and by its presence welds the irrational into a plan.

Finally, there is the role of the barber and the barber's wife. When the envoys set out with the dowry, the barber is one of them. At the subsequent ceremony, the barber's wife cleans the courtyard, makes a diagram, and sets out the ingredients and the pitcher. The barber's wife carries the basket and the mattock to the field for the earth digging. At the digging of earth from the well she carries the large basket used at the ceremony and herself digs out the earth. It is she also who crushes the turmeric and makes the paste for the anoint-ment ceremony. When the boy is about to set out, it is the barber's wife who cuts his nails and carries out a tray to the litter. The bar-ber goes to summon the party after its arrival and assists the bride-groom from the litter. The barber's wife cuts the nails of the bride and her mother under the wedding canopy and reddens their nails. The barber again acts as ambassador and informs the bridegroom's party when to come with the presents. He also summons the bride-groom for the final rites. When the bride is leaving for her husband's house, the barber's wife carries her to the litter and presents her with the water for spitting. At the immersion of the leavings, it is the barber's wife who carries the basket.

The reason for this important role is possibly their normal function in the family. The cutting of hair and nails makes them physically intimate with the household. They dispose of fragments of the body and have thus a fundamental physical relation. No other messenger, ambassador, or agent could, therefore, be more proper. On the basis of this relation they weave in and out of the action, "sewing" the various parts into a vivid and compulsive pattern. With their inflated power, their enhanced supernormal role, they display that element of strangeness which in the last analysis marks the ritual as a work of art.

SYNOPSIS OF THE MARRIAGE RITUAL

SELECTION AND BETROTHAL

Preliminaries

In essentials, a Kayasth marriage has much in common with an English marriage of the sixteenth century.[15] Like the Elizabethan form, it is arranged by the parents of the boy and girl. It assumes that both are strangers[16] and excludes love as a basis. Like an Elizabethan marriage, it takes place on the fringes of the girl's puberty and while her character is pliable. A passionate comprehension of each other by two adults may result from the marriage but it is not the beginning of it. Like an Elizabethan marriage also, its object is the procreation of children and particularly the provision of the father with a son. Above all, the marriage is the joining of two persons and the union of two families.

These assumptions form the basis of the ritual and around them the caste constructs a web of approved practice. This practice derives from traditional Hindu ritual and expresses Hindu attitudes and beliefs. But the ritual of one caste is never the same as that of another and within the caste, no two subcastes marry in quite the same way.

In the following account, I have described the system as current in the Srivastav subcaste in the Sadr subdivision of Shahabad; variations will be found in other subcastes and in other subdivisions, but for the purpose of this book to notice in detail every difference is unnecessary.

Selection. The marriage process starts when a girl reaches the age of twelve to fourteen. Her parents or guardians look around for a boy who is four to six years older, whose character and status seem suitable, and whose family are likely to accept a proposal. They consult their friends, relatives, and family priests, and in due course a suitable boy is selected. In some cases one or two marriage seasons elapse before a boy is found and when this happens anxiety becomes acute, the standards are lowered, and the marriage may even take place with a boy younger than the girl.

The comparison of horoscopes. As soon as a likely boy is found, the priest or the family barber asks for a copy of his horoscope. This is compared with the horoscope of the girl and if the two tally, the girl's father goes to the father of the boy and tells him his mind. The boy's father then has the horoscopes examined by his own priest and in the presence of the two fathers the priest declares whether the union will be happy. If the horoscopes agree and the union promises well the priest is given a small present by the girl's father and the marriage talks start. In cases where the horoscopes differ widely, the girl's father abandons the matter and searches elsewhere; but where the clash is small, the matter is often arranged with the priest and the talks are allowed to go on.[17]

Inspection of the girl. Once the stars are shown to be benign, the next step is the assessment of the girl by the boy's family. Enquiries concerning her economic position, her father's status in society, her own education, character, and physique are made and a maidservant, a female relative, or a younger son are sent to interview her and report. When the envoy arrives, he is welcomed by the girl's family and ushered into a room where the girl is sitting by a screen. To gauge her intelligence and voice he asks a few simple questions and so that he may judge her gait and color, she walks over and offers him betel. From the hand which passes him the betel, he gauges whether she is dark or fair. When the inspection is finished he gives her some money for buying sweets. This present ranges from five to two hundred rupees according to the boy's status. If the envoy is a woman, she inspects the girl's face and makes the same tests observed by the man.

Discussion of the dowry. The envoy then reports. If the report is favorable, the boy's father announces his approval of the marriage and the stage of discussing the dowry (*tilak*) is reached. For settling the dowry, the boy's father makes a demand. This is countered by an offer by the girl's father and the final amount is reached by higgling. If the report is unfavorable, the boy's father remains silent and makes no further move. The girl's father concludes from the silence that the match is off and begins to look elsewhere.

The encircling ceremony (barachhā). When the dowry has been settled, an auspicious day is fixed for the ceremony of preliminary engagement. The object of this ceremony is to put a circle around the boy in order to restrain him from opening marriage talks with anyone else. It is a preliminary rather than a final engagement, since although it restrains the boy from marrying anyone else, it does not bind him to marry the girl.

To perform the ceremony, a Brahman, a barber, a Bari, a Kandu, and a male member of the bride's family go over to the boy's house. The Bari, who makes leaf plates and cups, and the Kandu, who makes hearths, are taken as ceremonial relics from the days when parties had to camp in the open on the way. When they arrive, a barber summons the neighbors to the boy's house. The relatives assemble and a square pattern enclosing some unboiled rice paddy, betel leaves, nuts, some red powder, curd,[18] clarified butter,[19] country sugar, flowers, and cow dung is marked out on the ground. The boy is then washed and dressed in a red coat and a red hat is put on his head. The coat and hat are sometimes borrowed but must never have belonged to a dead boy. Similarly, a coat with black stripes must be rigorously avoided as both death and blackness will mean bad luck. The boy then sits on a shallow stool in the square and faces east. The family priest purifies him by sprinkling water and reciting charms. Unboiled rice is thrown over him and an image of Ganesh—the elephant son of Shiva—is made from cow dung and water. The ingredients within the square are offered to the image and the bride's party puts a token sum in the boy's hands in advance of the larger sum to be given later. The boy then rises and salutes the party and after giving the barber some food and fixing a date for giving the dowry, the girl's party returns.

The amassing of the dowry. A period of acute anxiety now follows. In almost all Kayasth households, the amount of dowry is pitched higher than the family can afford and land has to be mortgaged and relatives pestered before the due sum can be raised. When, at last, the cash is collected and cloth and ornaments have been brought, a small exhibition is held. The relatives and neighbors are called in to view the articles; their praise or criticism affects the dowry's final composition.[20]

The journey with the dowry. The dowry party is then formed. This usually consists of five dowry-bringers, each of different castes. The leader is a Brahman and the remaining four are chosen for the different functions they perform. A barber goes with the party to shave the Brahman and rub his legs with oil, a Kahar to serve him, a Kandu to collect fire wood and make a hearth, and a Bari to make leaf platters for food. They also carry the dowry and guard it on the way. The party leaves the bride's house early in the morning and if they reach the boy's village before sunset, they wait in a mango grove outside and go to the bridegroom at twilight.

The reception of the dowry-bringers. When the party arrives the boy's father asks them what kind of journey they had, offers them water for their feet,[21] and gives them sweet sherbet to drink. The dowry ceremony then follows.

The Ceremony of the Dowry

Preliminaries. For this ceremony the following arrangements are made. The barber's wife sweeps and cleans the courtyard and marks out a square with flour or powdered rice. Inside this square she puts a

small pitcher and a large and a small lid. The large lid is heaped
with rice or barley while some melted butter and cotton wick are put
in the small one. The small lid is later put on top of the large one.
In addition, mango leaves, *kush* grass, unboiled rice, betel, nuts, curd,
country sugar, camphor,[22] vermilion powder, cow dung, a low stool,
and some cotton flowers are put on the square. The Brahman then
casts an eye over the ingredients, and the bridegroom and the dowry-
bringers are then marshaled in.

The bridegroom, who is dressed in red, sits on the square facing
east while the dowry-bringers sit opposite him on a mat. Part of this
mat laps over into the square. Everything is now ready and the Brahman begins by flicking the water over the square with mango leaves.
As he does so, he recites prayers asking the earth mother to give the
boy a place to sit. The boy sits on the stool and rice is thrown over
him. He washes the Brahman's feet and powder, rice and curd are
put on the foreheads.

The marriage pitcher is then prepared. The bridegroom pours water
into it, adds a coin and a nut and then puts the two lids on its rims.
The cotton wick is lighted and is turned to the west.

The Brahman next models the cow dung into two cylindrical shapes.
One of these stands for Gaurī, the wife of Shiva, while the other
represents her son, Ganesh. The object of the images is to bless the
ritual by associating power and prosperity with it.

The pitcher-worship follows. The Brahman holds the pitcher up,
sprinkles red powder on it, mutters some mantras and puts it down.
With this act, the preliminaries finish and the way is clear for the
presentation of the gifts.

Presentation of the dowry. For this a large dish is touched with the
pot and set before the boy. Some rice is put in his hands and as the
dowry-bringers offer the articles, they brush them one after another
against the pot and put them in his hands. The boy puts the articles
in the dish and, as his hands fill, the coins clatter down. With the
clatter of the coins the women who are standing by in a band break
out into various kinds of wedding songs such as these:

I

In a new pot the curd was made
With a pinch of nectar
O bridegroom, eat it up
And rove the paths and shops.
A great rani asks you
Who graced your heart with sandal?
She who is my mother
And he who is my father
They graced my heart with sandal.

2

Plaster the court with cow dung
Mark out the square with elephants' pearls
For Rām must come and grace it,
His head dazzles with the wedding hat
His brow flashes with sandal
His ear glitters with gold
His brow flashes with sandal
His dress bedecks his body
And the sandal flashes on his brow.

As they sing, they crowd around him and make the blessing gestures (chumāwan). They put a handful of rice in his hand and an ornament over it and sing a song of blessing.

3

With rice and bright green grass
Is the daughter being blessed,
The mother is touching her
And giving her blessing.
"A hundred thousand years

May the bridegroom live
May he live as long as the world
And rule like the moon in the night."

Then they take him to the room which will be used as a bridal chamber *(kohbar)*. Here the boy bows down and puts the rice near a wall. Passing on to the family shrine, he bows down and then comes and salutes the women and his male relatives. The dowry-bringers and the guests are now given a feast and the women sing songs for the groom's party *(jewanār)* as well as bawdy songs known as *gālī*. Later the guests are given betel and, if the family is well-to-do, some dancing girls are brought in.

Fixing the wedding day. Early the next morning, the priests of the two families consult each other and fix the wedding day. The Brahman of the boy's family writes the date on a piece of paper, smears some turmeric on it, and ties it with a turmeric-colored string. The paper is then tied up in a turmeric-colored cloth along with some paddy, the fine grass called *dūb,* and turmeric. After receiving presents the dowry-bringers leave for home bearing the bundle with them. When they reach the bride's house, they report to the girl's father and put the bundle in the family shrine.

THE WEDDING PRELIMINARIES

The Starting Rite

With the presentation of the dowry, the stage of negotiation ends. The interval between this and the elaborate main wedding rites may vary according to the convenience of the two families and the need to choose an auspicious month and day. As the chosen date approaches the marriage begins to move towards its climax.

The first step at the girl's house is the auspicious *sāgun* ceremony. This begins the wedding process by sanctifying the girl and putting her into a special isolated state. In this state she will remain until the wedding is over.

The *sāgun* rite takes place about a fortnight before the wedding. The family priest chooses a day. A square is marked in the courtyard. The girl sits on a low stool and the bundle containing a piece of paper inscribed with the wedding date is untied. As this goes on, the female neighbors and relatives sing rounds of songs, including five *sāgun* songs and five songs to Shiva.

When the piece of paper has been taken out, the girl's hair is taken down. All her ornaments and bangles are removed and only her nose ring is left. Her hair is combed and parted. Her eyes are rimmed with collyrium and her limbs are rubbed with a paste called *bukwā*.[23] While rubbing is going on, the women sing:

4

> Of wheat and oats is the paste
> And mustard is the oil,
> The daughter
> > Is sitting to be rubbed.

> Oh the sweetheart of her father
>> Is sitting to be rubbed.
> That darling one
>> Is sitting to be rubbed.
> The mother comes to smear her
> With a bangle in her hand,
> The daughter
>> Is sitting to be rubbed.

When the rubbing is over, an old but very white sari with no black on it is put on her and some turmeric is smeared on one of its edges. This sari will be worn on the day of annointment and during the intervening period the girl will not wash herself. When she has put on the sari, some rice and an ornament are put in her hand and her mother and relatives then do the blessing gestures over her.

The dedication for the wedding. The girl, after going to the family shrine, bowing before the great Hindu gods *(devas)*,[24] and offering the rice, is then fed while the other women are rubbed with oil. A meal follows and the party then disperses.

From the day following the first rites, the women of the house gather in the evening to sing. They always begin with songs of Shiva's marriage and certain other auspicious songs *(mangal)*. They then sing spells to protect the betrothed *(jog, tonā)* and end with *jhūmar* songs. From then onwards singing occurs nightly until the wedding is over.

The Digging of Earth

The sanctifying preliminaries. The next stage is the ceremony of the digging of the earth *(matkorā)*. This takes place either five or eight days before the wedding and is generally done either in the early morning or the evening. A large basket is procured from a Dom, or sweeper. A blessing gesture is performed over it with the stone roller used for crushing spices and it is then set down in a sacred square.

The girl's mother then goes over to where a member of the leather-worker caste, a Chamar, is standing with a drum. She puts some vermilion on the drum, adds some rice, and arranges five betel leaves at five places. She then holds out her sari and the Chamar knocks the drum so that the rice and betel leaves fall in her lap. This rite, which is known as the worship of the drum (*manar-pūjā*), is done five times and is repeated by the other women. As they do it, they sing:

5

>His legs were worn out
>With bringing the drum
>Her sari was wetted
>In giving the blessing.

The procession to the field. Betel, a nut, a copper coin, and some rice are then tied up in a small bundle. This is put in the big basket with a paste made of turmeric and flour (*aipan*), vermilion powder, and five small baskets as well. Five women then lift the basket on to the head of the barber's wife and, to the sound of the drum, the women stream out to a field in the outskirts of the village. The drummer leads the line. The barber's wife comes next with a mattock on her shoulder and the girl's mother follows with a pot of water. As they walk, they sing.

6

>O Cuckoo, where is the jungle
>Where you lived?
>And where is the jungle
>Where you've gone?
>Where is the door
>Where you dance with joy?
>In Nandanban you stayed,
>To Brindaban you've gone.

Whose is the door
Where you dance with joy?

The excavation. When the band reaches the field, the mattock and the girl's mother are sanctified with vermilion, five hand-marks[25] are dabbed with *aipan* on the mother's back, and she makes five little cuts on the ground. With each cut a little earth comes out. This is scraped together, five hand-marks of *aipan* are put on it, vermilion is added, and it is then distributed among the five small baskets and the single large one. As the earth is being dug the women sing:

7

Take up the yellow earth,
O yellow earth
It is with you
That the wedding will go on.

The mother then rinses the mattock with the water from the pot and ties some of the earth into a corner of her sari. As the women troop back to the house, bawdy songs directed at the mother and the drummer are sung.

The dedication of the rice. When the band reaches the house, five women bless the large basket by waving a curry-roller over it. The basket is then set down in the sacred square. Some unboiled rice is then put in a rice mortar and five women clasp a rice-pounder and pound the rice up with it.[26] It is pounded five times and put in a winnowing fan. As they pound, the women sing

8

Pound the rice, gypsy, pound the rice
In her mortar pound the rice
"Sister, I'm pounding it,

> Pounding it, pounding it.
> The pounder is lost
> And I'm looking round for it.

When the pounding is over, the rice is carefully put away—to be taken out on the wedding day and cooked in the marriage bower. Similarly the earth is carefully taken up, sprinkled with water by five women, and stored in a corner of the court. As they sprinkle they sing to invoke the ancestors:

9

> O Grandfather, send your wife
> To damp the earth.

The earth is kept in the corner until a day or two before the bridal day. It is then mixed with more earth and made into hearths on which the bridal rice is cooked.

From the earth-digging day up to the wedding certain songs are sung each night, the mother wearing the same clothes each night and joining the singing.

Erection of the Wedding Canopy

Five, or sometimes three, days before the wedding, a bowerlike canopy (*marwā*) is put up in the girl's house.[27] The relatives and neighbors assemble. Nine green bamboos are cut and on the end of each the family priest ties a dozen mango leaves with sacred *munj* grass. He then measures the girl's forearms and breaks a stick to their exact length. With this stick he marks out a square. A hole is then dug in the center and the male members of the family lift up the center pole and set it in its place. It is roofed with thatching grass and bamboos, the bamboos being tied with strings of *munj* grass. As they perform this joint family act, the women sing:

10

O father, raise the wedding canopy,
My king comes
Screen me with a cloth.
O mother, paint the bridal room,
My king comes
Screen me with a screen.

The Anointing Ceremony

The digging of earth from the well. The anointing ceremony is done
either on the same day or two days later. A plough, a green bamboo
stick, and some green mango leaves are assembled in the marriage-
booth. These are all tied together with grass string and are placed in
the center. A band of women then set out for a well. The barber's
wife takes *aipan,* vermilion powder, and a mattock; on her head she
carries the large basket used in the digging ceremony. A drummer
beats a drum and as they leave the house the women sing songs of
the open air *(koilar.)* Out at the well, the girl's mother touches the
plinth with *aipan* and gives it five vermilion marks and then pours
some water on the ground. The wet earth is dug out by the barber's
wife and put in the basket, and as they surge back the women sing.
Under the canopy the damp earth is worked into a small mud platform by a Brahman priest with a plough.[28]

The preparations. A new pitcher is then brought in by a potter's
wife and after the blessing gestures have been done the girl's mother
takes it into the bridal chamber. Here the women smear it with fresh
cow dung and after that it is formally brought out by the barber's
wife and set down under the wedding canopy. The usual ingredients
are then assembled. The priest takes up his position and the girl is
then brought in.

The anointing. When she comes in, the priest first sprinkles some
rice on a low stool and seats her on it. She puts her hands on the

marriage-pot and the latter is then lifted onto the platform. The priest
fills it with water and the girl drops into it a copper coin, a nut, and
some rice. The ceremony of building up the pot follows. Mango leaves
are put on its rims. A lid of heaped up rice is put on the top and
over it a smaller lid with cotton wicks burning in butter.

When the pitcher has been finished, Shiva's consort Gaurī and her
son Ganesh[29] are worshiped and the turmeric paste is prepared. The
barber's wife crushes it on a curry-stone and mixes into it some turmeric brought from the boy's house by the dowry-party. This paste
in which both houses are united is then put before the priest.

A long series of repeated gestures follows. The priest takes five
mango leaves and some *dūb* grass in his hand, dips them in the turmeric, and lightly touches the girl's head, shoulders, knees, and feet.
He does this five times. Each married male member of the family
follows making the same gestures. Finally the male neighbors who
are married do the same. By this the girl is increasingly sanctified
and, at the same time, slowly, gently, and irresistibly absorbed into
the community of the wedded. As each man finishes he puts a small
coin in the pot of turmeric and goes away. As the ceremony is going
on, the women sing:

11

    The flower-girl sowed the turmeric
    The father buys it
    The mother buys it
    They put it on the head of the girl,
    They smear lovely turmeric on her brow.

The courtyard is now empty of men and the women swarm in to
rub the turmeric paste on the girl's body. One woman rubs her hands,
another her back, and another her legs and all symbolically absorb
her in a single mass anointing. As they rub on the turmeric they
sing:

12

Flower-girl, O flower-girl
You are my sister-in-law.
Where did you get this turmeric?
Frail is my daughter
And she cannot bear the paste.

After the paste has been put on her body, oil is put on her head and the women sing.

13

Oil-girl, O oil-girl
You are my sister-in-law.
Where did you get this oil?
Frail is my daughter.
And she cannot bear the oil.

Rice having been put in the girl's hand, a bangle or bracelet is passed over it, so that the rice is pressed more deeply in her palm, and blessing gestures are performed over her. Water is then sprinkled around her and in this sanctified state of purity she is lifted up and carried into the bridal chamber. Further anointings on the three succeeding days up to the wedding maintain her in this condition. On the wedding day she comes to the final rites in a state of isolated purity, already sanctified in marriage.

At the House of the Bridegroom

The digging of the earth. Action in the boy's house parallels the preliminaries in the girl's. The earth-digging ceremony is observed and the earth is formally taken from a field and placed in a corner of the courtyard.

The anointing with turmeric. Similarly, at the time the girl is being sanctified, the boy is also smeared with turmeric. The plough, bamboo stick, and mango leaves are erected in the bower and the pitcher is formally set in place. Then, before these symbolic witnesses, the turmeric is rubbed on.

Preparation of the wedding presents. The day before the wedding, a series of sweets are made and put into baskets covered with red cloth. Diagrams of a boy are painted on the cloth with gram powder and the baskets are marked with vermilion. Five packets of vermilion powder are also made up and twisted in red paper.

At the same time, the ornaments for the bride are counted and listed. A red sari, a red skirt, and a red blouse are made ready for the bride and new saris are brought out for her relatives. Each is duly labeled and wrapped up in red paper.

The feast of the five bachelors. A farewell feast is then given to the caste men and five young unmarried boys join with the bridegroom in taking food. This signals his departure into marriage, for until the feast he is still a bachelor, but after it, the rites will quicken, his bachelor state will be sloughed off, and he will enter the new state of marriage.

Washing the bridegroom. After the feast, a small trench is dug. The boy squats over it and water is poured on him. As the water runs through his hair, it is caught in a pitcher and this water is taken with the party when it goes to the bride.

Dressing the bridegroom. The wedding garments, consisting of a turmeric-colored dhoti, red stockings, red shirt, red turban, and a long wrap made from the muslin offered in the dowry, are then spread out on a bed and a tailor comes and dresses the boy. He squats on a leaf plate in the sacred square while his mother sits by him on a low stool. A flower-girl then comes in with two marriage hats, the larger of which is put on the mother's head and the smaller on the boy's.[30] The barber's wife cuts their nails and reddens their feet. The boy's mother then closes his eyes, cuts the nail of his little finger, and paints it. Her brother puts five mango leaves in her mouth, a cloth is put over the boy, and he bites each leaf in turn and spits the pieces

into her hands. Having wrapped the stalks and a little rice up in a
mango leaf, she fixes an iron ring over the packet and ties it to his
right wrist with a piece of cotton. Her brother then gives her a rupee
and pours water on her hands, then she rinses her mouth five times.
After this the boy throws a little rice on the leaf plate, goes to the
family shrine, makes reverence to the gods and then enters his litter.

The final blessings. As the boy gets into the litter, a band starts up,
the drums beat, and a cornet squeals. The barber's wife picks up a
metal plate on which rice, curd, sugar, betel, five lights, five pieces
of cow dung, and a curry-roller are arranged. The boy's mother marks
his brow with curds and rice, rims his eyes with kohl,[31] and presents
him with the shallow iron case in which the kohl is kept. She splits
a wick and a piece of cow dung into four parts and tosses them in
four directions. Waving the curry-roller over him, she makes the
blessing gesture.[32] Other women follow and, as the blessings go on,
they sing:

14

Under is the *kadam* tree
Above is the *bel*.
O mother, bless the lovely boy
And your eyes will be soothed
And your heart will be calmed.

The mock suckling. When the final blessings are over, the mother
covers his face with her cloth and pretends to breast-feed him. She
pours some water into his mouth with a pot and the boy spits it out.
She then crawls under the litter, backwards and forwards, five times,
the women inciting the litter-bearers to put the litter down and trap
her. Having thus safeguarded his path, she comes out. The other
women follow and crawl under the litter five times in turn. When
the crawling is over, the litter-bearers and servants are fed, the party
gathers, and the bridegroom starts on his journey. The women follow
the litter for about a mile to a fixed point in the village where all

bridegrooms halt. There they give the boy some water and after that
they return.

The Vigil at the Boy's House

The conjuring of the bride. After the boy's party has left, the women
disperse, but in the evening come together again. The bridal pitcher
is put in the square. The lamp with four wicks is lit on it and the
whole is shrouded in the large basket which was used at the earth-
digging ceremony. The mother then sits motionless on a low stool
while a sister-in-law *(gotinī)* dabs her toes with vermilion. As she
does so, the women sing:

15

> Do not wave your hands
> Or a girl who waves her hands will come.
> Do not say a word
> Or a girl who talks will come.
> Do not wink your eyes
> Or a girl who winks will come.[33]

The domkach. The party then relaxes and a noisy pantomime called
the *domkach*[34] is performed. The central figures are a woman who
has been stung by a scorpion, a woman with a dhoti tucked up, disguised as a country doctor, and four women in mixed clothes who
act as maidservants and messengers. The woman knows she has been
stung but cannot say where, and a careful test proceeds, mounting
gradually from her toes, heels, and shins to her knees and thighs. As
her clothes are pulled back the excitement and merriment come to a
climax. The bite is discovered in the most improper of her parts and
she declares she is cured. The pantomime then dissolves into singing
and chatter.[35]

The test of the wicks. At intervals during the night the basket is
taken off the pot and the lamp is examined. If the four wicks are

still burning separately, it is judged that the wedding is still going on; but if they have fused into one, then the vermilion has been given and the wedding is over. Once the wicks have fused, the party disperses and the women go to their beds.

THE WEDDING DAY

Preliminaries in the Girl's House

Preparations. When the wedding day dawns, the courtyard in the girl's house is washed and plastered. Plantain posts are put up at the entrance. Leaves of the *ashok* tree are tied to them and, if the family can afford it, marquees are erected. Outside the village, a mango grove is made ready for the boy's party.

Invocation of the ancestors. The barber's wife puts a curry-stone[36] and roller inside the courtyard and assembles the normal ingredients. The priest takes his seat. The girl's mother and four married women in red saris, and with fresh vermilion powder on their brows, squat round the curry-stone. In their saris they put a little rice, a cloth is spread over their heads, the wick on the pot is lighted, and the girl's mother picks up some rice from the square and drops it on the curry-stone. As she does so, the women of the house invoke the ancestors and household

16

O Brahmā, Vishnu, and Shiva Maheshwar,
Today you must heed my bidding.
O gods who live in the courtyard,
Today you must heed my bidding.
O grandfather who lives in heaven,
Today you must heed my bidding.
And your wife who lives with you,
She too must heed my bidding.
O cat who lives behind the hearth,
You must stay away today.

O wind and rain and clouds,
You must stay away today.
O black ants and red ants,
You must stay away today.

As each ancestor is named, the women sprinkle a little rice on the stone. When all the rice has been dropped, the four crouching women press in on the mother and she starts to grind the rice.

17

The married woman sits to grind
And may he live
For a hundred thousand years.

The ground-up rice is then put in a leaf cup, the leaf cup is folded and placed near the pitcher, and the curry-stone and roller are turned over and pressed into it.[37] As this is done the women sing:

18

"*Ghasar ghasar*" sounds the rice,
My darling, she is a mare
And he is a rider
And this one's a groom,[38] my darling.
The mare has stumbled
And the rider's fallen
And the groom is laughing,
My darling.

The women are then given some balls of sweetmeats and in return they offer presents of small coins.

The feast of the five virgins. A meal is cooked under the wedding canopy, the hearth being made of the special earth brought on the earth-digging day. Five platters of *palās* leaves are set out and rice, pulse, curds, and sugar are circled round the girl's head before being placed on the ground. The bride and four other virgins then sit in the bower and eat the meal together. As they eat, the women sing auspicious songs. When the meal is over the bride is given a nut to chew. But instead of chewing it she keeps it in her mouth until the evening when she takes it out, splits it, and gives it to her husband. The leavings from the meal are collected, tied in a bundle, put up in the roof under the tiles, and left there for a year from the wedding.

The worship of the feet. When the feast is over, the ground under the canopy is cleaned and the normal ingredients reassembled in the square. The bride's father washes himself and puts on a turmeric-colored dhoti, a new sacred thread, and a yellow turban. His wife also washes and puts on a red sari and blouse. The two then sit on stools under the canopy and the father's wrap is tied to the mother's sari. The family priest recites the worship of Gaurī and Ganesh and at the end is given a turmeric-colored dhoti and some money. Similar presents are made to the family priest and the more senior relatives; the women sing:

19

At a good time was he born
At a good time was she born
They worship the guru's feet
For on a lucky day were they born.

The offering of butter. From the worship of the feet, the bride's parents move over to the bridal chamber, the bride and the priest going with them. At the door the priest models ten little strips of cow dung and places five on each side of the door. The father puts butter on them with mango leaves and the mother dabs them with vermilion. While they do this, the women sing:

20

O green parrot with a red beak
What did you see under the canopy?
I saw him pouring butter,
I saw her with her hair loose
I saw a daughter holding her parents' hands.

They then go into the room and the priest props seven strips of cow dung against the wall, and pastes a piece of turmeric-colored cloth over them. The father puts some butter on it and the mother adds some vermilion. Some powdered wheat is then mixed with water and five strips are put beside the cow dung. These are offered to the ancestors.

After this, the bride, her parents, and the priest come outside, the wedding canopy is hung with fancy finery and the house waits for the bridegroom.

The Bridegroom's Arrival

Worship at the door. As the bridegroom's party arrives, it settles into its camp. It stays there for some time and then at an auspicious hour after dusk the barber goes to summon them and the Bari, clad in a long coat and a turban and wielding a sword, comes out from the girl's house to usher them in. The bridegroom's party slowly comes into motion. Any elephants, camels, and horses that have come are led out and, with a band blaring into the night air, the bridegroom is borne in the sky, gun shots[39] banish evil spirits, and groups of women sing marriage songs.

When he reaches the girl's house, the boy finds the door closed and on the ground before it are a painted square and a pot. The barber helps him down from the litter and seats him on a stool. The bride's father washes his feet, preserving the soiled water in a dish. The family priest performs the worship of Gaurī and Ganesh and the cash portion of the dowry is then given to him. While the worship is being done boys of the two parties challenge each other to sing songs of "obstruction" (rokā) and any boy who fails is hooted out. At the same time the women sing:

21

Sweep clean your lane, O Lāl,
Your bridegroom son-in-law is coming.
I called the party early
But it's coming late
With a lamp I scan his face
And his eye squints.

22

Sweep clean your lane, O Lāl,
Your bridegroom son-in-law is coming.
For sitting he needs a red bed
For playing he wants a field
For chewing he asks a ripe betel
For eating, he needs sweets.

When the worship is over and the payment has been made, the bridegroom and his party go back to their camp.

The invitation to the bridegroom. The bride's father then collects a small party. Food and sweets are loaded on the heads of five girls of the Kahar caste, each load being wrapped in red cloth. Lights go ahead and a band plays. The party goes across to the boy's camp and in the camp they chat for a little. Members of the two parties sing *gajals* and presently the father wraps a pot of water in a handkerchief, makes a present of cash to the boy's father, and invites him formally to his house. The boy's father having signified acceptance by touching the pot, makes a round of the boy's party, inviting each in turn to give his consent in like manner. The family barber then takes charge of the boy's marriage hat and the water in which he was washed. The band collects again and to its blaring sounds the girl's father gathers his party and returns.

The Preparation of the Girl

Washing the bride. When the girl's father is back in the house his sister digs a small trench with five cuts in the courtyard. A plank is put across it and the bride is brought out and made to squat. As she sits, the women sing.

23

> Who dug a tank and made the steps?
> Who brings water for Rām to wash?
> King Dasrath dug the tank and made the steps
> Rām's mother brings water for him to wash.

Her body is then rubbed all over with gram and turmeric and rinsed with water. Her mother pours water on her first, followed by the married women. Finally the water from the bridegroom is splashed over her. As the water is being poured the women sing.

24

> Fast flows the stream
> Where Gaurī is washing,
> Washed are her sins, and her life
> Is fruitful with good works.

The women then dry her and wrap her in a turmeric-colored sari.

Circling the bride's sari. As the girl is being dressed, a second turmeric-colored sari is brought out and in it are tied a nut, rice, and a copper coin. A rite known as "Circling the Flower" (*kusum lorhan)* is then performed by moving the sari round and round the head of the girl. As the sari circles, the women sing:

25

> Do not grow a flower father!
> Who will pick its blossoms?
> Picking its blossoms, a thorn will prick
> And the sun will wear you out.

The attack on the evil eye. The women then crowd round the girl, each woman holding a sweet in one hand and some mustard in the other. A fire is kindled in a little pot and each woman puts a sweet in the girl's mouth and circles her head with mustard.[40] As she completes the circling she tosses the mustard into the fire and the women sing:

26

> With mustard the mother circles her head
> O look that there is no evil eye
> Take care that there is no evil eye.

When the rite is finished, the fire is knocked out and the girl stomps on the pot and breaks it.

The nail-cutting. She is then conducted under the canopy and seated by the mother's side. Her mother dons the marriage hat brought by the bridegroom's party and puts its fringes on the girl's head. The barber's wife purifies the mother by cutting her fingernails and painting them red. The mother puts her hands over the bride's eyes and the bride puts her hands on top of them. The barber's wife cuts the nail of her little finger and colors it with henna. The girl's eyes are then freed and the mother circles a silver coin over her head and puts it in a pot. The women who have been standing by crowd in and do the same.

Swallowing the tamarind. A rite known as *imlī ghotanā*, the swallowing of tamarind, then follows. In this there is no tamarind and no swallowing, but instead the mother's brother puts five mango leaves into the girl's mouth. The girl bites off the stalks and puts them into her mother's hand, and her uncle throws the leaves away. When the five stalks are in the mother's hand, her brother puts a coin of silver or gold on them and rinses them with water. The mother raises her hand to her lips and throws the water away. The brother pours water four more times and each time the mother solemnly raises her hand, moistens her lips, and tips the water away. The stalks and some rice having been wrapped up in a mango leaf, an iron ring is fixed onto it and the packet is tied to the girl's left wrist with a piece of cotton. The brother then steals out of the court but not before the women have playfully manhandled him, rubbed curds on his face, and twitted him.

27

On golden clogs walks the brother,
Where is the sister to swallow the tamarind?
Brother, you haven't a rupee
And they are putting you to shame.
Brother you might have pawned
Your wife's red sari
Had you brought a gold mohur
And swallowed of the tamarind.
What a name you would have won!

The women then make blessing gestures over the girl and lead her into the nuptial chamber.

Painting the bridal chamber. On the wedding day, this room is washed and plastered with cow dung. A white square is painted on the wall with rice-water; in it a diagram resembling an elephant and rider, called "Shiva Mai," is drawn. White hand-marks are imprinted on the walls and in this religious and protective atmosphere the girl waits.

The Gifts from the Bridegroom

The family barber goes to the bridegroom's party and suggests that the ornaments and clothes for the girl should now be sent. The bridegroom's eldest brother accordingly gets them ready and accompanied by a small band of attendants he comes over to the girl's house. When he arrives, he is given a seat outside while the courtyard and wedding canopy are cleared of women. The bride's hair having been combed and parted, her eyes are rimmed with black and a ring is put in her nose. She is taken under the wedding canopy bower where she sits huddled beneath a sheet.[41] As she is taken in, the women sing:

28

The marriage party sits beneath the eaves
The father brings his little doll,
That little doll with its lovely form
How it charms the party.

The bridegroom's eldest brother is now ushered in and is given a seat before the girl. As he sits, the women sing:

29

The wedding basket and the marriage hat
The joy of the bride
Have come,
And with her I am sitting in the square.

The ornaments and clothes having been produced, he touches these to the pitcher and the bride and lays them on some leaf-plates. When the offerings are over, he takes a betel leaf, some curd, and some rice. For the first and last time, he touches the girl by putting them on her brow. While the ornaments are being offered, the women sing:

30

Under the canopy you show
The ornaments you borrowed,
O brother, to have so little shame!

As he touches her they sing:

31

Today her brother touches her
And decks her in gold,
He is calling her his own
He is dragging a lame leg
He is winking a blind eye.

The boy throws some rice over her and, taking his party with him, returns to the bridegroom. The women bless the bride again and conduct her to the nuptial room.

The Wedding Climax

The blessing of the bridegroom. The time is now ripe for the bridegroom to appear. The barber is sent to summon him and in a litter he is carried to the house. He is put down under the canopy and the girl's mother and her relatives come to anoint him. The mother rims his eyes with kohl, puts a mark of curds on his forehead, and offers him a folded betel in which the nut chewed by the bride has been inserted. She circles his head five times with the curry-roller. The other women follow and when they have all circled him they withdraw.

The giving away of the bride. The bridegroom is seated on a stool which the priests of both families have touched with the pitcher. The girl's father is called and sits by his side. The father's shawl is then tied to a turmeric-colored string which is carried into the nuptial room and tied to the sari of his wife. The barber's wife then brings the bride in and places her in her father's lap, and as she does so, the women sing:

32

On the thatching grass the father sits
The girl with loosened hair is in his lap,
O praise the thighs that bore a girl
Who holds her with a pearl in her hair.
O praise the thighs that bore a son
Who brings him in a golden litter
To the wedding.

The worship of Gaurī and Ganesh is next done and all the ancestors of the bride and bridegroom are invoked.

The girl's youngest brother then takes his stand with a pot of water. Her father puts his hand on the bride's and places the bridegroom's hand on top. The priests recite charms and the brother pours the water on them. As he pours, the women sing:

33

O brother, pour the water
In a single jet,
If the jet is broken
You will lose your sister.

The father now places the girl's hand in the boy's and the bride's priest asks the bridegroom if he takes the girl as his wife. The boy answers yes and swears by all the gods and goddesses that he will be true to her, that her comfort will be his happiness and her sadness his sorrow. The boy's priest asks the girl if she will be a devoted wife and to this the bride nods assent. She is then picked up and put on her father's lap while the bridegroom is dressed in a new turmeric-colored dhoti given by her father. He also receives a cloth in which some parched paddy has been tied. They stand one behind the other with the girl in front of the boy. The boy stretches his hands out, links them with the girl's,[42] and the bride's youngest brother sprinkles some parched paddy on them. The bridegroom then bends down and touches the girl's toes with his hands and as he does so the women sing:

34

Mix the parched paddy, O brother,
For she is your sister.
Touch the girl's toes, you little bastard
For she is your wife.

A circumambulation of the wedding canopy follows—the bride and bridegroom going around it seven times; while, as they go, three or four men of the party pass the bridegroom's shawl around it seven times.

The vermilion mark. The rites culminate in the act of placing the mark of vermilion powder on the bride's forehead. The Brahman knots the boy's shawl to the girl's sari and ties a copper coin, rice, and a nut into the knot. The boy stands before the girl. He puts the vermilion on the pitcher and on the mud models of Gaurī and Ganesh; then he dabs vermilion on her forehead five times. As he does so, the women sing:

35

Father, father, I call
But my father does not answer,

> Against my father's will
> The groom marks me with vermilion.

With this rite the wedding is complete and the union irrevocable.

The blessing of the hair. The bridegroom now sits on the girl's left and the priests utter charms and pelt them with rice. The men depart from the courtyard and the women file past the pair, putting rice and ornaments in their hands and exchanging marks of vermilion powder with the bride. The blessing gestures come to an end, water is sprinkled on the pair,[43] and they rise to their feet.

The way to the bridal chamber. The bridegroom then walks toward the bridal chamber with the bride following. Her sister is standing at the door and as the boy arrives, she sings a song to bar his entry until he sings a song of love *(gajal)*.

36

> I will not let you cross the threshold,
> Son-in-law,
> For you've had your mother
> And you've slept with your sister.

While the bridegroom is struggling with a *gajal* the women tease him:

37

> If his father can read
> He'll read one out,
> If his father's a drummer
> He'll beat a drum
> If his father can't read
> He'll push his way in.

At last the *gajal* is sung to the girl's satisfaction, the door is opened, and the pair go in.

The ritual in the chamber. On entering the chamber the bride dabs vermilion on the mural diagrams. The bridegroom takes off his marriage hat. A stone is put near the wall and he is asked to worship it as his family deity.[44] Finally a plate of curds and country sugar is brought. The bride secretly takes some first and the bridegroom eats what is left.[45] As he eats, the women sing:

38

O wife I'll eat your leavings
I'll be your slave
I'll stay by your bed
I'll fan your cheeks
I'll look at your parted hair,
And if I find it bare
I'll jail your father
And buy you a spangle.

The unrobing of the bridegroom. The bridegroom is then led into a room where he is safe from the women. His wedding trousers and stockings are taken off and he is given a special wedding meal. He finally gets into his litter and is borne back to his camp.

THE POST-WEDDING RITES

At the House of the Bride

The wedding breakfast. The following morning, the bride's father invites the boy's party to a meal of food cooked in fat *(pakki rasoi)*. The party comes and when the bridegroom has been given further presents he allows the meal to start. As the party is eating, the women sing bawdy songs *(jewanār* and *gālī)*.

The wedding dinner. A second meal is given in the evening. At this, the food is not cooked in fat *(kacchā)*. While the morning's feast was in honor of the bridegroom, the evening's is in honor of the bridegroom's father. Here also the presentation of sufficient cash is necessary before the bridegroom's father will accept and much time goes in higgling before a final sum is reached. When at last the party has gathered at the girl's house, the bridegroom, his father, and a few of the nearer relatives sit under the wedding canopy while the rest of the party is grouped on the verandas. The girl's father sits beside the boy's father and the two who are now relatives by marriage *(samdhi)* formally dine together. As the meal proceeds, the women continue to sing bawdy songs. The bridegroom and his party go back to their camp.

The piercing of a mock ram. Early the following morning a ceremony of anointment known as *ābtauni* is performed. The barber's wife makes a thick paste of turmeric, mustard oil, and powdered barley. The bride and bridegroom are placed in the wedding bower, her sari is knotted to his shawl, and the women gather to rub the hands and feet of the pair with the paste and give them presents of money. As they rub, they sing auspicious songs. The barber's wife then gathers up the fragments of paste and models them into the shape of a toy ram. The boy is given a stick and is told to run it through the ram.[46] He does so and is given a gift. Gestures of blessing are made over the pair and they are taken to the nuptial chamber. Here they are given some curds and sugar, the knots are untied, and the bridegroom returns to his party.

Destruction of the wedding canopy. The rites are now almost over. To symbolize their completion, the parties assemble under the canopy for the last time. The lamp in the marriage-pot is lit. The bride is screened with a cloth. The worship of Gaurī and Ganesh is again performed. The boy's father then gives the bride a costly sari and some ornaments while his relatives offer their presents. The bridegroom's father then unties some knots in the roof of the canopy and shakes one of the bamboo poles. This signifies that the rites are successfully accomplished and that the canopy may now be dismantled.

The union of the families. A distribution of betel, dried fruit, perfumed oil, and rose water follows. The leaders offer each other betel under the canopy and the two fathers embrace. They then join the main party and all the relatives of the boy. The party now gets ready to depart and the boy is carried home in his litter while the child-bride stays behind.

The filling of the houses. In families where the girl is mature she goes home with the boy. But before she mounts her litter, certain rites are necessary. The boy goes with her into the nuptial chamber, stands behind her, puts his arms through her armpits, and links his hands. The girl touches his hands and rice is sprinkled on them five times. Each time the rice is put, he tosses it over his back. The women then ask him whose house he is "filling." If he answers correctly, he will say the house of his father and mother-in-law, that is to say the joint house of the two families, but if he is in an impish mood, he first says the house of his father and mother and only after remonstration modifies it to the house of his father and mother-in-law. "Filling the house" means "filling it with children."

The marriage sermon. When the boy has answered properly, he salutes his mother-in-law and the other women by touching their feet. He then goes outside and does a round of the men, starting with his father-in-law and touching the feet of all the older male relatives. As he stands before him, the father-in-law gives him a short marriage sermon, telling him to live well and giving him his blessings. The boy now mounts his litter and is carried back to his camp, where, starting with his father, he does a similar salutation of his relatives.

Parting from the parents. The girl is then prepared for the journey. She puts on a going-away dress consisting of a red sari and a shawl. Her feet are painted red. Rice, turmeric, and a little cash are tied into her sari and the women streak the part of her hair with vermilion. She embraces each of her relatives, all the time weeping bitterly, and the women embrace her back and weep as well.[47] The barber's wife then carries her to the litter and places her on a red quilt. Rice is put on the bed and she is also given a box filled with vermilion powder, some curds, butter, and mustard paste. The litter-bearers then swing the litter on to their shoulders and start on their journey to the boy's house.

The spitting of water. When the litter has left all the village houses behind, the bearers put it down and the barber's wife, accompanied by women of other castes—a cup-maker, a sweeper, a washerwoman, and a palanquin-bearer—presents the bride with a pot of water. She takes a mouthful and spits it on the ground. She then tips the five women and the litter solemnly goes on. With the spitting of the water, her connection with her home is finally severed, the old ties are put aside, and she goes on to the new life of the bridegroom's home.

At the House of the Bridegroom

Entry into the boy's family. When the two litters reach the boy's house, they are put side by side and the bridegroom sits beside the bride. The women of the house come out, carrying vermilion powder, country sugar, and a pot of curds. As they come, they sing:

39

Smiling my boy comes home
And I wonder why he's come,
That strumpet of a mother-in-law
Has cast a spell
And I wonder why he's come.

The bridegroom's shawl is tied to the sari of the bride. The women mark the bride's head with vermilion and the bride marks theirs in return. A dab of curds and sugar is put on the bridegroom's brow and blessing gestures are done on the pair.

Walking on the baskets. Five large baskets are then brought out and are put like stepping-stones between the litters and the nuptial chamber. In each basket is some rice. The bride alights from the litter and stands in a basket. The bridegroom follows and stands beside her. He then takes the pot of curds from the women, puts it on the bride's head, and with the bridegroom steadying the pot with his hand they walk along the baskets into the chamber.

The absorption of the bride into the house. In this room five pots have been assembled containing the fundamental requirements of a household—oil, salt, turmeric, butter, and curds. When they enter, the bridegroom puts butter on the walls while the bride dabs them with vermilion. The bride then takes each of the pots in her hands—by this gesture linking herself to the fundamentals of the household. After this the bridegroom eats a little curd and sugar and the knot in their clothes is untied. He salutes his mother and the other women and goes out.

The process of identifying the bride with the house is now carried further. The mustard brought by her in the litter is made into a paste and the wife of the family barber rubs it on the boy's feet. This links her yet again with her husband. She is then carried first to the kitchen and then to the store room, in each of which places she touches the food and offers a rupee. She is brought back to the nuptial chamber, where she eats a meal with four other girls, and when the meal is over she bows low before the women and offers them a rupee.

The immersion of the refuse. On the fourth day after the wedding, the bridegroom is washed in the water from the marriage-pot. The bride's hair is rinsed with gram powder and, after she has taken a bath, she is dressed in a red sari. The refuse of the ceremonies is then put in a big basket—the same as that in which the virgin earth was brought from the field. Oil, vermilion, and pastes of turmeric and flour *(aipan* and *bukwā)*, as well as sweets, are added. The bridegroom, his mother, and the other female relatives now go in a body to the Ganges or, if the Ganges is too far, to a neighboring tank. The barber's wife carries the basket on her head and a drummer beats a drum. At the Ganges, the refuse is tipped into the stream.

The removal of the leaf wristlets. The party then returns home where the final ceremony is performed. A diagram is made in the courtyard and five cakes of wheat and five of gram are arranged, one of each at each corner and one in the center. The bride and bridegroom sit in the square and the family priest does the worship of Gaurī and Ganesh. When this is done the women sing:

40

Incense and prayers are over
The smoke rises to the sky
And all the gods are pleased.

The wristlets are then untied from the wrists of the bride and bridegroom and are tied round the mother's neck. The mother wears them for a day and then keeps them in a safe place. After the wristlets have been removed, the bride and bridegroom are fed and the meal is served to the agnates. The night that follows is the night of consummation *(sohāg ki rāt)* and the bridegroom sleeps with the bride.

MARRIAGE SONGS

THE TECHNIQUE OF
BHOJPURI POETRY

The main formal elements in Bhojpuri songs are their free musical rhythms. The lines in a song usually conform to a rough base but there is scarcely ever any strict metrical pattern. The number of syllables is determined by the tune and the meaning, and a line is stretched or shortened at will. Moreover the value of a syllable is rarely constant and whether it is equal to one, two, or four syllables depends on its place in the line and the way the line is sung. In the general elasticity of their rhythms, the songs are forerunners of modern European poetry.

Apart from this freedom of rhythm, an overriding element is rhyme. In English poetry, the same rhyme rarely covers more than three lines. In certain Bhojpuri songs, a single rhyme may cover all the lines, as in song 168:

Sāwan umari ghumari ghan barase tarase jiyā sakhi ri mor
Mor ki boli katāwan lāge mor ki boli katāwan lāge dādur kare ghanghor
Sāwan umari ghumari ghan barase tarase jiyā sakhi ri mor
Piu piu kari ke papiharā bole jhingur ki jhankor
Sāwan umari ghumari ghan barase tarase jiyā sakhi ri mor
Tāl talaiyā nadiādi sab umari chali chahun or
Sāwan umari ghumari ghan barase tarase jiyā sakhi ri mor
Rimi jhimi bund bahat chahuāin nahin āyi chitchor
Sāwan umari ghumari ghan barase tarase jiyā sakhi ri mor.

In some songs continuity of rhyme is made possible by repeating the same words, as in song 60, while in other songs, although there is no rhyme, the same effect is secured by refrains, as in song 57, where assonance is even more general and the beauty of the song comes from the echoing repetition of the vowels *a, i,* and *e*.[48]

> *Malahoriā ke galīe nikalu mere lāl bane*
> *Ab karo maurī kā mol sahānā lāl bane*
> *Malhorin hai manmohanī more lāl bane*
> *Ab dulahā kamal kā phul sahānā lāl bane.*

> *Dulahā ke sire pagiyā bhalā sobhe*
>> *Dulahin ke sobhe anār kalīyā*
> *Phulwariyā men derā girā de re*
>> *Bhalā bagiyā men derā girā de re*
> *Dulahā ke mukhe birā sobhe*
>> *Dulahin ke dānte mīsīyā re*
> *Dulahā ke ange jorā bhi sobhe*
>> *Dulahin kā sobhe choliyā re*
> *Bagiyā men dulahā ke seje dulahin sobhe*
>> *Dulahin ke sange lokaniyā re.*

In this poem rhyme combines with assonance, but in other songs assonance is the sole agency for a verbal effect as in song 111:

> *Motar gāri re chalābe sāri ratiyān*
> *Sone ke thāri men jebanā parosalon*
> *Jei lehu re motarwālā rasiā*
> *Sone ke geduā gangajāl pāni*
> *Pi lehu re motarwālā rasiā.*

Of the Chinese Book of Songs, Arthur Waley writes:

When in 1913 I first began to read them, it was not as documents of the past that they interested me. It was simply as poetry that I read the songs, and strangely enough, perhaps even more as music than as poetry. For though

I soon distrusted the Confucian interpretation, I had nothing to put in its place and was often forced to accept the songs as meaningless incantations. And yet as I read, there sprang up from under the tangle of misconceptions and distortions that hid them from me a succession of fresh and lovely tunes. The text sang, just as the lines of Homer somehow manage to sing despite the barbarous ignorance with which we recite them.[49]

It is a similar singing quality in which rhyme, assonance, and rhythm are all joined which constitutes the major charm of Bhojpuri poetry.

SONGS OF GOOD OMEN
SĀGUN

Sāgun songs are sung at the ceremony which commences the period of sanctified waiting by the bride. The word *sāgun* means "the thing which happens first" and hence, by usage, omens—"the things which are noticed first."

41

Curds and fish
The first omen
And a betel leaf
With its stalk,
These are good omens
And fast approaches
The wedding hour
These omens, O Sītā,
Will bring him to your village
And fast approaches
The wedding hour.

"Him" is Rām, the bridegroom, and the meaning is that if these omens are taken, they will make the wedding hour come quickly.

E. M. Forster in *Abinger Harvest* gives a vivid description of betel *(pān)*. The importance of the stalk is that, if it is attached, the leaf will dry up less quickly.

Seeing curds, fish, or a betel leaf and its stalk are all good omens—curds because in an agricultural community they are of fundamental importance, fish because its prolific breeding means plenty, and betel because the gods eat it. Curds are regarded as particularly auspicious and a man may go out of his way to eat a little with some sugar and dab a little on his forehead before starting out on a walk or a journey.

DOWRY SONG
TILAK

42

Today the dowry comes from Janakpur
O Mother, take the dowry.
Today the dowry comes from Janakpur
O Mother, take the dowry.
"Father growls the dowry is too small."
Today the dowry comes from Janakpur
O Mother, take the dowry.
"Pick up the dowry and take it away
My boy will stay a bachelor."
Today the dowry comes from Janakpur
O Mother take the dowry.

This is a dialogue between the dowry-bringers and the mother of
the bridegroom. Janakpur is the family seat of the legendary King
Janak, the father of Sītā, Rām's bride.

THE MARRIAGE OF SHIVA
SHIVA KA BIWĀH

These songs relate to the marriage of Shiva and Pārvatī, another name of Gaurī, and are sung at marriages as emblems of what the married state should be. To the public, Pārvatī's marriage seemed disastrous, but to Pārvatī, Shiva was the ideal husband. Although the songs show Gaurī in attitudes that vary from rapturous love to a dull resignation, the marriage is extolled because it shows the wife's perfect devotion to the chosen husband, a devotion which triumphs over snakes and scorpions and ascetic manners.

Concerning the cult of Shiva, Russell and Hiralal write:

Shiva is a highly composite deity, having the double attributes of destroyer and creator of new life. His heaven, Kailās, is in the Himalayas according to popular belief. He carries the moon on his forehead and from the central one of his three eyes the lightning flashes forth. He has a necklace of skulls and snakes are intertwined round his waist and arms. And he has long matted hair, from which the Ganges flows. It seems likely that the matted locks of the god represent the snow on the Himalayas, as the snow is in reality the source of the Ganges; the snow falling through the air and covering the peaks of the mountains might well suggest the hair of a mountain god. . . . Shiva has thus three components from which the idea of death might be derived: First, his residence on the Himalaya mountains, the barren, lifeless region of ice and snow, and the cause of death to many pilgrims and travellers who ventured into it. Secondly, he is the god of the moon, and hence of darkness and night, which are always associated with death. In this light he might well be opposed to Vishnu, the god of the sun and day, and the source of growth and life; their association as the supreme two deities representing the preservation and destruction of life, would thus, to some extent, correspond to the conflict of good and bad deities representing light and darkness among the Zoroastrians. Thirdly, Shiva is a snake god, and the sudden death dealt out by the poisonous snake has always excited the greatest awe among primitive people. The cobra is widely revered in India, and it is probably this snake which is associated with the god. In addition the lightning, a swift, death-dealing power, is ascribed to Shiva, and this may have been one of his earliest attributes, as it was probably associated with his Vedic prototype Rudra. Whether Shiva obtained his character as a god of destruction from one only of the above associations, or from a combination of them, is probably not known. Two great forces lend the deity his character of a god of reproduction, the bull and the phallic emblem. The bull tills the soil and renders it fertile and capable of bringing forth the crops which form the sustenance of mankind; while the phallic emblem is worshipped as the instrument of generation. It is believed that there is a natural tendency to associate these two objects, and to ascribe to the bull the capacity of inducing human fertility as well as the increase of the earth. It is in these two attributes that Shiva is worshipped in the rural tract; he is represented by the emblem standing on a circular grooved stone, which is the yoni, and in front of him is a stone bull. And he is revered almost solely as a beneficent deity under the name of Mahādeo or the Great God. Thus his dual qualities of destruction and reproduction appear to be produced by the combination in him of different objects of worship; the Himalayas, the moon, the cobra and the lightning on the one hand, and the bull and the emblem of regeneration on the other. Other interesting characteristics of Shiva are that he is the first and greatest of ascetics and that he is immoderately addicted to the intoxicating drugs *gānjā* and *bhāng*,[50] the preparations of Indian hemp. It may be supposed that the god was given his character as an ascetic in order to extend divine sanction and example to the practice of asceticism when it came into favour. And the drugs, first revered themselves for their intoxicating properties, were afterwards perpetuated in a sacred character by being associated with the god. Shiva's throat is blue, and it is sometimes said that this is on account of his immoderate consumption of *bhāng*. The *nīlkanth* or blue-jay, which was probably venerated for its striking plumage, and is considered to be a bird of very good omen, has become Shiva's bird because its blue throat resembles his. His principal sacred tree is the *bel* tree, which has trifoliate leaves, and may have been held sacred on this account. The practice of Satī or the self-immolation of widows has also been given divine authority by the story that Satī was Shiva's first wife, and that she committed suicide because she and her husband were not invited to Daksha's sacrifice. Shiva's famous consort is the multiform Gaurī, Devī, Kālī, or Pārvatī.[51]

43

In a mottled dress
Shiva starts for his wedding
    Too young is Gaurī
    She cannot marry Shankar.
On his head no marriage hat
But a mass of matted hair
    Too young is Gaurī
    She cannot marry Shankar.
In his ear no pearls
But black scorpions
    Too young is Gaurī
    She cannot marry Shankar.
On his neck no pendant
But a necklace of snakes
    Too young is Gaurī
    She cannot marry Shankar.
On his body no wedding dress
But a smear of ashes
    Too young is Gaurī
    She cannot marry Shankar.
On his feet no stockings
But a cracked skin
    Too young is Gaurī
    She cannot marry Shankar.
With him no band
But a rattling drum
    Too young is Gaurī
    She cannot marry Shankar.
To the temple she goes
And bolts it from within
And there she worships
The image of Shiva

The sages gather
And try to advise her,
"O sweet heart of your husband,
This bridegroom
Is lord of the three worlds
Great is your luck
To get him as a husband."
  Too young is Gaurī
  She cannot marry Shankar.

44

Beating comes the drum
Waving comes the flag
From where comes the bridegroom
Swaying as he comes?
And everyone is staring.
"With Gaurī
I will fly in the air
With Gaurī
I will go deep underground."
Better is it
That she stays a virgin
Than weds an ascetic.
"Daughter,
Seeing his matted hair
How scared you will be,
Seeing his ashes
You will get a fever,
Seeing his other wife
You will burn in your heart.
How can you ever
Care for his kingdom?"
"For me, his matted hair

Will be sandalwood,
For me, his ashes
Will be my vermilion,
For me, his other wife
Will be a companion—
So I'll take
To his kingdom.
Mother,
Don't fly in the air.
Mother,
Don't plunge into water.
Mother,
Don't go deep underground—
Mahādeo is in my fate
And can't be altered.
Rise up, O Mother,
Don your red silk
And do the blessing rite—
Lord of the three worlds
Mahādeo I must marry."

In the first part of this poem, Gaurī's mother is speaking and is
threatening to remove Gaurī rather than agree to her marriage. In
the second part, Gaurī is replying.

The line "his ashes will be my vermilion" means that so long as
Shiva lives he will smear himself with ashes and the ashes will therefore be a sign that he is living and that her married state (sohāg) is
continuing.

Red silk is worn when prayers are being offered or a form of worship is being done.

45

"High is your brow, Gaurī
And your eyes are bewitching,

With that ascetic husband, daughter
What kind of life did you lead?"
"Mother, you knew what he was
When you made the marriage,
Why do you ask
How I am living?
Were you my brother's wife
I would have told you straight,
But I blush to tell you
Acts of shame."
"Daughter, if you tell your brother's wife
She will only laugh at you,
Daughter, if you tell me
I shall keep it in my heart."
"Mother, my hands are worn
From grinding *bhāng*,
Mother, from grinding thorn apple
My body's eight parts reel,
Mother, the scorpions breed
In his matted hair,
Mother, the snakes hiss
In the strands of his tresses,
Mother, this is how I lived
With my ascetic husband."
"I will dose myself with poison
I will burn my body
I will become an ascetic
For dooming my daughter thus"
"Mother don't take poison
Don't burn yourself—
What is fated must be."

The elder brother's wife *(bhaujī)* is often of a similar age to a young wife and is therefore a natural confidant. The phrase "the body's

eight parts" occurs constantly in popular Indian poetry. Compare the
Baiga poem:

> Under the pipal tree there is a little bed
> She is wearing many bangles; her breasts are large.
> On all eight parts of her body she wears red necklaces.
> She is slender and beautiful; she stands beneath the pipal.
> Beside her is a little bed.[52]

The association of snakes and scorpions with Shiva's hair are visual—the snakes resemble long tresses and the scorpions shorter curls.
For a similar association compare the Chinese poem:

> That knight of the city
> Dangled a sash cut so as to hang.
> That lady his daughter
> Curled her hair like a scorpion.[53]

46

> To her garden goes Gaurī
> To pick some blossoms
> Mahādeo calls
> As he rides on his ox,
> "Whose is this innocent?
> Whose is this darling?
> Who was it told you
> To come to this garden?"
> "My father's innocent
> My mother's darling
> My brother told me
> To come to the garden."
> Her basket he's broken

And he's scattered the blossoms,
Gaurī goes sobbing
Back to her home
Gaurī is sitting
With a sick heart.
Her mother asks Gaurī,
"Why are you brooding?"
"I went to pick blossoms
In the father's garden,
On his ox rode Mahādeo
And started to call me.
My basket he broke
And scattered the blossoms
And sobbing I came
Back to my home."
"Oh you little fool,
You stupid little one,
Your own husband it was
And you didn't know him."

47

After twelve years comes Shiva
And from Gaurī demands a proof,
She bows to the sun
And the sun disappears.
"The test of the sun
I will not accept,
Give me instead
The test of the basil."
She touches the basil
And it sheds its leaves.
"The test of the basil
I will not accept,

Give me instead
The test of the Ganges."
Into the Ganges
She dips her hand
And the Ganges
Turns to sand.
"The test of the Ganges
I will not accept,
Give me instead
The test of fire."
She flicks the fire
And the flame withers.
"The test of fire
I will not accept,
Give me instead
The test of the snakes."
She picks up a snake
And it coils on her hand.
"Let the earth split
And take me in
But the words of Shiva
I cannot bear."
"*Bhāng* and thorn-apple
I grind and drink,
Stupid and fuddled
I ask for proof."

This poem refers to Shiva's return after his absence for doing aus-
terities. The tests are designed to prove Gaurī's chastity.

MORNING SONG
PRĀTKĀLI

Such morning songs may also be sung at night in the period between the settling of a marriage and its performance.

48

With her child in her lap
The doe is moaning,
"Away I would fly
But for my children,
O tell me a jungle,
Where I may hide?
On one side is a fire
On another is a trap
On a third is the hunter aiming.
What jungle can I hide in?"
A cloud puts out the fire
A wind carries off the trap
A snake bites the hunter
And God saves her,
O renounce the world
And meditate on God.

TURMERIC ANOINTMENT
HALDĪ

Haldī songs are sung while the bride and bridegroom are being rubbed
with turmeric paste.

49

> In a gold cup is the *haldī*
> In a gold cup is the *haldī*
>> And the barber holds it in his hand,
>> The girl's father
>> Offers the *haldī*
>> And *jai jai* shouts the crowd.
> In a gold cup is the *haldī*
> In a gold cup is the *haldī*
>> And the barber holds it in his hand,
>> The girl's uncle
>> Offers the *haldī,*
>> The girl's uncle
>> Offers the *haldī*
>> And *jai jai* shouts the crowd.
> In a gold cup is the *haldī*
> In a gold cup is the *haldī*
>> And the barber holds it in his hand,
>> The girl's brother
>> Offers the *haldī,*
>> The girl's brother
>> Offers the *haldī.*

In the song the *haldī* is *kanch* or virgin *haldī,* which is offered to a
man only once in his life and can never be offered to a widower. *Jai,*
which the party of wedding guests shouts, means "victory."

SONGS OF ORNAMENTATION
SEHALĀ

Sehalā songs are sung in the boy's house before his departure for the wedding and particularly just after he has put his wedding garments on. The *sehalā* is the groom's marriage hat with its fringe, the strings and tassels that dangle in front of his eyes.

50

Bridegroom with the red beads
The red beads,
Wearer of a red fringe,
Bridegroom
Bridegroom with the red beads
The red beads.

51

In all his escort
Is the bridegroom red.
Red is his fringe
Red are its tassels
    Wherever one looks
    He is red
Red is his gold
Red is his earring
Red are his garments
Red is the sash
    Wherever one looks
    He is red

Red are his socks
Red is the paint
Red is his horse
Red is the bridle
    Wherever one looks
    He is red
Red is the litter
Red is the screen
Red is the bride
And red are her features,
In all his escort
Is the bridegroom red.

52

Red, red, everywhere red.
Red is the bridegroom
Red is the bride
Scarlet beyond the veil,
Red is the fringe
Red are the tassels
Scarlet beyond the strings,
Red is the wedding dress
Red is the shawl
Scarlet beyond the shawl,
Red are the stockings
Red is the paint
Scarlet beyond the henna—
Red, red, everywhere red.

"Scarlet beyond the veil" means that the face which lies beyond the veil is also scarlet, while "scarlet beyond the henna" means that the feet which have been dyed with henna are themselves scarlet. The word for "scarlet" in the poem is *gulanār*, scarlet as the flower of the pomegranate.

A Ukrainian custom also links red to a wedding. In this region the horses pulling the car in which the bride is taken to the bridegroom's house are adorned with red ribbons; her mother seizes hold of their bridles, leads them to the road, and wishes her daughter a good night, while the other women who accompany her sing:

> "We have laid her upon a white bed,
> She has herself desired a red
> Beet-root for her white body."[54]

53

> Bridegroom,
> Oranges are in your hands,
> O marriage crown
> That shines on his head,
> Trinkets are on your strings,
> O ring
> That shines in his ear,
> Trinkets are on your pearl.
> O garments
> Shining on his body,
> Trinkets are on your sash.
> O stockings
> Shining on his feet,
> Trinkets are on the henna.
> O lovely girl
> Who shines on his bed,
> Trinkets are on your veil.
> O bridegroom,
> Oranges are in your hands.

In Bihar and other parts of India oranges are a common image for breasts, and so, in an indirect way, for a woman. Prokofiev's "The

Love of the Three Oranges" uses it and the symbolism also occurs in Wycherley's *The Country Wife*:

(Re-enter Mrs. Pinchwife running with her hat full of oranges and dried fruit under her arm, Horner following.)

Mrs. Pinchwife: O dear bud, look you here what I got see!

Pinchwife: And what I have got here too, which you can't see. (Aside, rubbing his forehead)

Mrs. Pinchwife: The fine gentleman has given me better things yet.

Pinchwife: Has he so?—(Aside) Out of breath and coloured! I must hold yet.

Horner: I have only given your little brother an orange, sir.

Pinchwife: (To Horner) Thank you, sir. (Aside) You have only squeezed my orange, I suppose, and given it me again; yet I must have a city patience. (To his Wife) Come, come away.

Mrs. Pinchwife: Stay, till I have put up my fine things, bud.

54

Friend, come and see
How grandly he is dressed.
On his head a marriage crown
Fine the tassels,
In his ear a ring
Fine his pearl,
His garments shining on his person
Grand his sash,
His socks adorn his feet
Fine the henna,
His bride charming on his bed
Fine her veil—
Friend come and see
How that princely youth is dressed.

55

"On your head shines the spangle,
Charming are your eyes
Today I am yours,"
At the boy smiles the bride.
"In your nose shines a ring,
Fine is its circle
Today I am yours,"
At the boy smiles the bride.
"On your neck a fine necklace,
Lovely is the pearl
Today I am yours,"
At the boy smiles the bride.
"On your wrist shines the bangle,
Grand is your bracelet
Today I am yours,"
At the boy smiles the bride.
"On your feet shines the anklet,
And bright are the bangles
Today I am yours,"
The bride smiles at the boy.

56

Twitters a sparrow,
"The dust has been shaken
The red tent is pitched
At the door of the father of the bride."
Twitters a sparrow,
"The dust has been shaken
The elephant shifts
The elephant shifts
At the door of the father of the bride."
Twitters a sparrow,

"My husband is king of love
And I am the queen of his palace."
Twitters a sparrow,
"My husband is a string of silk
And I am the pearls."
Twitters a sparrow,
"The drum is sounding
The fiddle is playing
A girl is dancing
A girl is dancing
At the door of the father of the bride."
Twitters a sparrow
Twitters and twitters a sparrow.

The meaning is that dust has first been shaken from the red tent
and then it has been pitched. The sparrow is the yellow-throated
tūtī, Gymnorbis flavicollis.

57

The head of the bridegroom
Shines with a turban
The bride charms
With a small pomegranate
  Camp in the garden,
  Halt in the grove.
The mouth of the bridegroom
Is bright with pān
The teeth of the bride
Flash with black powder
The body of the bridegroom
Is grand in his dress
The bride charms
With the slip for her breasts

The bride adorns
The bridegroom's bed
The bride dazzles
With the maid of the bridegroom
    Camp in the garden,
    Halt in the grove.

Anār kaliyā is a pomegranate fruit not yet fully formed, and as such a very common term for the breasts, though it is sometimes also used for a tiny jewel worn on the forehead. This symbolism is common in India and elsewhere. A description of an Arab beauty states that the eyebrows are thin and arched, the mouth small, the lips a brilliant red, the teeth are like pearls set in coral, while the forms of the bosom are two pomegranates.[55] In the ballads of Eastern Bengal, the pomegranate flower is used as a simile for a girl's beauty. "She was a thing of joy like a star that appears from the evening cloud, or a pomegranate flower gently touched by the wind."[56] Crooke notes that through its brilliant scarlet flowers, red juice, and numerous seeds the pomegranate is also connected with fertility generally.[57]

58

Father, O father,
Adorn the elephants
Adorn the horses.
The uncle, the uncle
Is grouping the party,
On the bridegroom the brother
Is putting the sandal,
The father's sister
Pencils the eyes,
The sister, sister
Sprinkles the saffron—
In a cloud of perfume
The party starts.

59

In your garden, O flower-girl
On the brow of the bridegroom
Sandal looks well.
In your garden, O flower-girl
Comes an elephant and howdah.
In your garden, O flower-girl
Comes the party on camels.
In your garden, O flower-girl
The mouth of the bridegroom
Flashes with betel,
On the bed of the bridegroom
Dazzles the bride.
In your garden, O flower-girl
On a bed of flowers
Comes the elephant and howdah,
In your garden, O flower-girl.

60

Pass through the gardener's alley
And haggle for the marriage crown,
O you prince of a bridegroom.
The flower-girl is a lovely girl,
O princely bridegroom,
And the bridegroom is a lotus bloom,
O you prince of a bridegroom.

61

The bridegroom alights
Who is his guardian?
The bridegroom fidgets
With his pink shawl

Who is his father?
The bridegroom's father
Straightens the pink shawl
Who is the bridegroom's mother?
The bridegroom's mother
Fans him with her cloth.

62

The father prepares
A set of wedding clothes,
The sister's husband
Prepares another—
Look at the lovely groom's walk,
Look at his lovely face.

63

The grandfather
The grandfather
Must put on the crown
For I am a bridegroom today.
The grandmother
The grandmother
Must cover my head with the end of her sari
For I am a bridegroom today.
My aunt's husband
My aunt's husband
Must dress me in my wedding clothes
For I am a bridegroom today.
My aunt
My aunt
Must cover my head with the end of her sari
For I am a bridegroom today.
My father

My father
Must group the marriage party
For I am a bridegroom today.
My mother
My mother
Must cover my head with the end of her sari
For I am a bridegroom today.

Covering the head with the end of the sari refers either to the swallowing of the tamarind or to the pantomime of breast feeding which
occurs just before the bridegroom's journey.

64

I have scoured the fair,
Where is my husband?
In house after house
Looks the grandmother,
From market to market
Searches the grandfather,
Where is my husband?
From house to house
Searches the mother,
From market to market
Searches the father,
Where is my husband?
From house to house
Looks my brother's wife,
Market after market
Searches the brother,
And I have scoured the fair—
Where is my husband?

SPELLS TO PROTECT THE BETROTHED
JOG

Jog songs are sung from the day of anointment to the wedding day, that is, in the period when the bride and bridegroom are believed to be in particular danger from the evil eye and from evil spirits. This period is also the time when other girls may seek to cast a spell on the bridegroom, the bride herself may cast a spell over her husband in order to make him pliant, or the bridegroom himself may cast spells.

65

Shine on the spangle
Shine on the pearls
On this lucky night, O moon,
Shine in the sky,
On this bridal night, O moon,
Shine in the sky,
On this night of the bridegroom
Shine, O moon.

66

I will put it in the turban
I will put it in the spray
I will put it on the bridegroom
That magic of the mother,
On the bridegroom I will put it,
That magic of the mother.

I will put it in the pearl
I will put it in the ruby,
That magic of the mother,
It will work on the bridegroom,
That magic of the mother
On the bridegroom, the bridegroom.

67

With a spell I set a crown
And the bridegroom is enchanted,
O my mother, my spell.
In the grove of flutes
I made magic
O my mother, my spell.
On the bank of the Jumna
I made magic
O my mother, my spell.
On the way to the chamber
I made him mine
O my mother, my spell.

68

Thorn-apple leaves are flat, mother
The bridegroom is fuddled
With the grandmother's magic,
Fuddled, fuddled
Is the girl's lord,
But I don't know
How the magic took effect.
Vermilion on her head
Her eyes' black lids
Sandal on her breasts,

But I don't know
How the magic took effect.

Poems 65, 68, and 69 are "chain" poems of which the first link
only has been translated. In poem 65, for instance, the verse is repeated over and over, substituting in turn the various ornaments for
the spangle; while in the present poem, the grandmother yields place
in turn to the mother, the boy's aunt, and all his female relatives.

69

In her grandmother's hamlet
She learns the art of magic,
The bridegroom is fuddled
By her grandmother's art.
The art of others
Is nothing, nothing,
The grandmother's art
Brings baskets of presents,
Fuddled, fuddled
Is the girl's lord.

70

I charmed the bridegroom's crown
The charm went round and round—
It mounted and sat on his head.
The girl who cast the spell
Was a rich man's daughter,
The girl who cast the spell
Was a darling.

71

Fish of the Makhdun pond
Come into the river and stream,

Yes, into the river and stream,
    O mother, my charm.
What kind of girl
Enchants my son
Enchants my son?
    O mother, my charm.
What lovely boy
Casts his net
Casts his net?
    O mother, my charm.

The meaning is that in her father's house the girl was enclosed as in a pond. When she came out into wider circles, she completely dazed the boy and he is now trying to get her.

72

Where is the fish
That comes of its own will,
O mother, my magic.
When comes the groom
Casting a net?
O mother, my magic.
Whose is the son
Who casts the net?
O mother, my magic.
Who is that lovely girl
Who casts her spell?
O mother, my magic.
The grandmother
Wise in magic
Has cast the spell,
O mother, my magic.
O sister, make a charm

That brings in a groom
As I sit at home.

   For a similar use of fish, compare Middleton, *The Roaring Girl*:
These are the lecher's food, his prey; he watches/ For quarrelling
wedlocks and poor shifting sisters/ 'Tis the best fish he takes.

73

On the magic day, O mother,
Who is the girl cooking
In the shell of a snail?
Who is the girl, O mother,
Feeding from the leaf of a tamarind?
O mother, who is the boy?
On the magic day, O mother,
Who is the girl cooking rice
In the shell of a snail?
Who shows me her alley?
Who is the girl
Who makes me leave my alley?
O mother, who is the girl
Who takes me from my mother's lap?
O mother, who is the girl?
Who puts me in her mother's lap?
O mother, who is the girl?

TONĀ

Tonā songs are supplementary to *Jog* and are sung during the same period.

74

On the turban I will put a charm
And on the spray of feathers,
O lovely husband,
I do not know a charm.
O my mother,
Why did you put a loving spell?
My mother
Does not know a loving spell.
O bridegroom,
Bind that loving spell
With a string of tears,
Tightly bind that loving spell.

75

The first charm
Your grandmother sent.
Yes yes
My beauty's darling,
Let the charm fall on the turban
O my young Krishna
Let the charm fall on the pearl,
O my bridegroom.

These chain songs would continue through the various items of attire (poem 74) and the relatives (poem 75).

SONGS FOR MARRIAGE
BIWĀH

Biwāh songs, like *mangal* songs, are sung throughout the wedding period and act as an incantatory background to the ritual.

76

Behind the father's house a cool wind
Stirs in the thick bamboo clump,
The father has put his bed in its shade
And is sound asleep.
Bending bending his daughter
Comes and upbraids him,
"With a girl not yet married in your house
How can you sleep so sound?"
"Sometimes I sleep, sometimes I wake,
Sometimes I worry over the dowry.
Daughter, until you are married,
I shall never sleep soundly.
Daughter, shake a mat
And welcome your father-in-law,
Worrying for your dowry
I cannot think what you should do."
"Father, how shall I make the bed?
Where shall I put the mat?
Can you ever get me to a husband's house?
The dazzling moonlit night
Is shining on my forehead."

77

The pepper leaves are thick
There's talk in the town,
"With an unmarried girl in his house
How can the father sleep?"
Hearing the talk, the father
Rouses himself and shakes his shawl,
He scans an almanac
Weeping he comes home,
"Vermilion is dear in the market,
And costly is the marriage mark
For only a marriage mark and vermilion
You leave your country, girl.
A brother and sister
Spring from the same womb
And drink to the full their mother's milk;
A brother inherits his father's wealth,
A daughter is sent to a distant land.
Oh play up the music, musician,
And sound a trumpet
Declare the family branch, O Brahman
For I will marry my daughter."
The bridegroom speaks behind the pitcher
And says to the fair bride,
"Do not spoil the rites
I will row your boat."
"O sailor, what is your boat made of
And what is your oar?
What bridegroom sails in the boat
What bride goes over the water?"
"My boat is of gold
My oar is of silver."
The bridegroom is the sailor
And the bride crosses the water.

78

What is the bed made of,
And what are the four legs,
How is it strung
And what bridegroom sleeps on it?
The bed is of gold
The legs are of silver
With silk is it strung
And Rām sleeps on it.
With a box of vermilion in her hand
And a white betel in her sari
Sītā sleeps with her husband,
Her eyes are closing in sleep
As she tosses and turns.

In this poem Rām and Sītā seem only to be Rām and Sītā but the
marriage context gives them a suppressed and added meaning. Beneath the name of Rām is the figure of the bridegroom and beneath
Sītā is the bride. The poem in fact is a form of saying "as Rām the
bridegroom sleeps and as Sītā the bride sleeps with her husband."

79

A bridegroom stands by a sandal tree
And proudly and loudly chews betel,
Over his head a cuckoo tells him
To spend the noon beneath the tree.
"How can I pass the noon, O cuckoo,
The time is right for my wedding.
Give me the boon, O cuckoo,
That my marriage hat will be golden."
"Load your dowry on bullocks,
Bring your bride in a litter."
"Cuckoo, as soon as I return

I will dress you in a sari
And put gold on both your beaks."

The Indian cuckoo is an auspicious presence at a wedding, since
its call is believed to waken desire.

80

Whence is the caparisoned elephant-cow
With red painted on her legs?
Whence is the pretty darling
With the jewel on his brow?
A father sends a letter to another,
"Will you stay in the northern wing
Or under the *bar* tree?"
A father sends a letter in return,
"Not in the northern wing, O father.
Nor under the *bar* tree,
But under the canopy
At the wedding of the girl."

81

Where has the builder come from
Who put up the palace?
Where has the king come from
To look at the palace?
Outside, the palace
Is like a roof of betel leaves,
Inside, the palace
Is like a painted picture.
O praise his thighs who begot a son
And with a gold umbrella
Brings him to the wedding,
O praise his thighs who begot a daughter

And sits her on his knee
With a neat ribbon in her hair.

In this poem the palace is either the nuptial chamber or the wedding canopy.

82

In whose river shines bright water,
In whose river are weeds,
In whose river are minnows,
And who is the bridegroom
Throwing a net?
In the father's river
Is bright and shining water,
In the brother's river
Are the weeds
In the father-in-law's river
Are minnows
And the bridegroom
Throws a big net.
A net he throws
A second time he throws it
And catches snails and weeds,
A third time he throws
And lands a young girl.
"O bridegroom, when I look at your teeth
The lightning dazzles
And your lips are clipped leaves of betel.
Looking so lovely, O bridegroom,
Why were you so long a bachelor?"
"My father sits in state,
"My brother tills the land,
My uncle trades in cumin seeds,

And so was I still a bachelor.
My father has left his sitting,
My brother has left the land,
My uncle has left his trade,
And now I can marry."

In European poetry and dreams, the image of the fish is often a symbol for the male organ. Compare the following poem by Federico García Lorca in which the knife (also a phallic symbol) merges into the fish.

With a knife,
With a little knife
Which scarcely fits into the hand,
But which penetrates thinly
Through the astonished flesh,
And stops at the place
Where trembles entangled
The dark root of the shriek.
And this is a knife,
A little knife
Which scarcely fits into the hand;
Fish without scales or river.[58]

Among the Nagas of Assam, a fish is also used symbolically but less as a phallus than as a male substitute. When a man wishes to marry, he goes to an old man of his class who is the father of many children and uses the well-understood formula, "I am going to fish today, come to my house in the evening." He goes and catches some fish and comes back to his father's house in the evening to find the old man and a number of friends waiting for him. He hands over the fish to the old man to carry, and walks behind him to the girl's parents' house. The fish is left and he and the old man are given a drink, but nothing is said about the marriage. In the morning he goes again to the girl's parents' house and is given a meal. If the girl's parents eat of the fish brought the day before it means that they agree to the marriage.[59]

In Bhojpuri and Uraon poetry, on the other hand, the fish is always female and an image of the fish is a symbol of the bride. The river is the father's house and the bridegroom in marrying the girl takes a fish from its river.[60] The fish, in fact, is social rather than sexual.

For "catching snails and weeds," compare Sir Edwin Arnold's translation of the Rajput ballad of Bhagawati:

> She quaffed one draught from her hollowed palm,
> And again she dipped it,—Hu-ri-jee!
> Then leaped in the water dark and calm
> And sank from the sight of them,—Hu-ri-jee!
>
> Sorely the Mirza bewailed and hid
> His face in his cloth, for rage to be
> So mocked: "See, now, in all she did
> Bhagawati fooled me!—Hu-ri-jee!
>
>
> Grieving the Mirza cast a net,
> Dragging the water,—Hu-ri-jee!
> Only shells and weeds did he get
> Shells and bladder-weeds;—Hu-ri-jee!

83

> Where grows the palm tree
> And where do the betel leaves grow ripe?
>   The handsome bridegroom feels sleepy.
> At his father-in-law's house
> The palm tree grows,
> In his father's house

The betel leaves grow ripe,
 The handsome bridegroom feels sleepy.
He chews betel
And goes to the canopy smiling
 The handsome bridegroom feels sleepy.
The bride smiles as she speaks,
"O my lord, show me your dazzling teeth."
 The handsome bridegroom feels sleepy.
"O bride,
How can I show you my dazzling teeth?
Mothers-in-law crowd the wedding canopy."
 The handsome bridegroom feels sleepy.
"O my lord, with the edge of my sari
I'll screen the crowd under the canopy
And I will join you in love."
 The handsome bridegroom feels sleepy.
"You and I will go to our room."
 The handsome bridegroom feels sleepy.

In this poem the palm tree with its coconuts is a symbol for the bridegroom and the betel leaves for the bride.

84

In the night the *bel* opens
In the night the *bel* blossoms,
The flower-girl puts out her hand.
"And now I will pick you,
Wait a little, O flower-girl."
"The buds are green
In the night my blooms will open
And then you may pick them."
Where was the bride born
And who has reared her?

What bridegroom is waiting to wed her?
"Now I can marry."
In Arrah was the bride born
And her mother reared her
The bridegroom is waiting to wed her.
"Now I can marry,
Wait a little, O bridegroom,
I am under my father.
When my father waves the holy grass,
Then you may wed me."

In this poem the *bel* (*Aegle marmelos*) is an image for the bride, the flower-girl is a symbol for the bridegroom, while picking the flower is the nuptial act.

85

Daughter, the day you were born
My womb was aching,
I did not fancy meat or fish
My womb was aching,
Daughter, the day you were born.
It was an August night,
The mother-in-law and the husband's sister
Refused to light a lamp,
Even my lord
Spoke to me roughly.
The day you are married, daughter,
The father's heart will be eased,
Grand will seem the birth
That brought the gods to our house.

The wedding is over
The red is on your head,
The dowry cost nine *lakhs*.

Break up the pitchers in the court,
Even on an enemy I wouldn't wish a daughter.

Had I known a girl was in my womb
I would have drunk hot peppers.
The peppers would have killed the child,
How free of cares I should have been!

A night in August *(Bhādo)* is notorious for its gloomy darkness. A similar attitude toward the female child is expressed by the Chinese poet Po Chu-i in a poem titled "Golden Bells":

When I was almost forty
I had a daughter whose name was Golden Bells
Now it is just a year since she was born;
She is learning to sit and cannot yet talk.
Ashamed, to find that I have not a sage's heart:
I cannot resist vulgar thoughts and feelings.
Henceforward I am tied to things outside myself
My only reward, the pleasure I am getting now.
If I am spared the grief of her dying young,
Then I shall have the trouble of getting her married.
My plan for retiring and going back to the hills
Must now be postponed for fifteen years![61]

86

Behind my house are many ponds
Lotus leaves ripple in the wind,
The bridegroom goes to wash his dhoti
And the bride asks him,
"Whose little pet are you
Whose darling son?
In whose pond are you washing

And where are you going?"
"I am the pet of my father
And my mother's darling
I wash in the pond of my wife's father
And I go for vermilion."
She puts on a petticoat
And speaks to her father,
"Search the country for a bridegroom
Who is washing in a pond."
She puts a string bed in the courtyard
For the bridegroom to sit on—
Bride and groom are as one.

———————

87

Sweeter than mango is tamarind, father,
And the *mahua* is in bud,
A marriage mob surrounds the house.
In an upper room is a gay door
And around the palace is the crowd,
The girl's father sleeps in the room.
"O father, how can you sleep so soundly
With the marriage mob at the gate?"
"I sleep for a while, I wake for a while
And often I brood on the dowry—
Cows and buffaloes, daughter,
Bullocks and fertile cows
I have given as dowry for my daughter
And still the son-in-law isn't content."
"Cows and buffaloes, father, you have given
But the son-in-law is piqued for a knife."
"Let the dawn come, daughter
And the market start,

When the bridegroom smiles
With a knife in his hand
And walks to his party
The crowd will leave the door."

The *mahua (Bassia latifolia)* is a tree bearing sweet fruits used in
preparing liquor; its budding means that the girl is ripe for marriage.
Although parting with her and paying her dowry is bitter like a tamarind, it is better and therefore "sweeter" than keeping her unmarried at home like a mango. "The knife" has obvious sexual implica-
tions.

88

Mounted on the high bank of the Ganges
The bridegroom sits chanting the god's name.
"When shall I see the garden and grove,
When shall I see the house of my wife,
When shall I see my bride,
That bride whose sight
Will soothe my eyes?
On the edge of the village
I shall see the garden and grove,
From the door
I shall see my wife's house.
Under the wedding canopy
I'll see my wife's sisters
And her brother's wife,
In the bridal room
Will wait the virgin girl."
"Whisper, O bridegroom,
A crowd sits in the bower,
Go on with the wedding
And let me go to the room.

I will point out my mother
With her yellow shawl
And yellow on her limbs,
That woman with her tear-filled eyes
That woman is my mother."

AUSPICIOUS SONGS
MANGAL

On the mountain the god rains
In Lanka the lightning glitters,
Is it King Dasrath destroying forts
Or is the king hunting?
No, the king isn't destroying forts
No, the king isn't hunting,
Rām's marriage is at Janakpur
And this is his marriage party.
When King Dasrath nears the village
His elephant trumpets,
At the elephant's beauty
The sun dims and the five limbs wither.
The mother climbs to the second storey
And wishes she had ten daughters
As she peers through the window,
"This daughter is my foe and my heart's pain,
For my daughter my town is looted
And my honor is brought low.
The wedding is over
Vermilion is on her head,
It is the time for the dowry."
She takes a pot from a room
And dashes it on the doorstep.
"Even on an enemy I wouldn't wish a daughter,
Cows and buffaloes

Bullocks and fertile cows
I have given
And Rām demands a pond in the dowry.
When my husband sits in a meeting
No one dares answer him,
Now my husband bends low
And says, 'Sītā is your maid.' "
The mother speaks from behind a pillar,
"Listen, my husband,
Now that your daughter is given away,
Of what use is
The pond on the family land?
When a girl leaves her village
The pond dries
The red ducks fly to the jungle
The lotus leaves shrivel."
"Daughter, bring a pandit
With a stalk of grass
And I will give the pond to you."
When the father made his gift
The pond filled with water
Gaily the red ducks sported
And the lotus leaves floated.
"Wash in the pond, daughter,
And dry your long hair on the bank
And when anyone asks whose pond it is
Say it is your father-in-law's."

The mother "wishes she had ten daughters" so that the display of
the wedding might be repeated ten times; but this is succeeded by
the reflection that "even on an enemy I wouldn't wish a daughter"—
so heavy is the marriage price.

The ruddy sheldrakes, or *chakai* birds, are an image of conjugal
felicity. The legend is that when Rām was searching for Sita, he

asked a pair of *chakai* birds whether they had seen her. They said no and, feeling that they were not sympathizing with him, he ordained that they should always be separated at night. For this reason the birds stay together in pairs by day and fly apart at night.

90

A cup of sandal
A case of betel,
O Rām, take the betel
From your mother-in-law.
    O mother in Janakpur
    I will give Rām my blessing.
The turban of Rām flashes on his head
Lovely is Sītā's sari
With its gold border.
    O mother in Janakpur
    I will give Rām my blessing.
The wedding suit of Rām
Shines on his body
Lovely is Sītā's vermilion,
Beyond all praise.
    O mother in Janakpur
    I will give Rām my blessing.
The stockings of Rām
Shine on his feet
Lovely Sītā's painted toenails,
Beyond all telling.
    O mother in Janakpur
    I will give Rām my blessing.

91

O father, seek for me a bridegroom
I am a grown girl

Find me a bridegroom, father
At whom the village will not laugh.
Go in the evening to Awadhpur
Straight to the door of Dasrath,
The young man will be playing
By the Sarju with the princes.
If you find him small
Do not be dismayed,
Little he may be but he is very wise
Among four brothers the blue one is my husband.
Get the green bamboos cut, my father,
And put up the green wedding bower,
Make the roof high
So that my husband need not bend his head,
Plaster the court with cow dung
And mark the square with elephant's pearls,
Put the rice on a gold pitcher
And light a ruby lamp.
The wedding is over
Vermilion is marked on my head,
It is time to go
Hurry and get me started, father,
How will my husband go?

92

From Awadhpur starts the party,
There is a stir in Janakpur
All the young and charming girls
Come to bless the blue face,
The sun god sits on the shaken mat.
The groom waits under the canopy
Janak lolls to one side,
The thatch is cut from the pond

Rām sits on Dasrath's knee,
And the sun god goes from view.
Sītā sits on Janak's knee
Lovely are all her sixteen parts,
Her friends crowd to greet her
Her mother weeps on her neck
Full of love her sister comes
Her mother holds her to her heart—
Contest for Sītā
The bow of Rām
Grand the father's fate.

"The blue face," i.e., the "bluish" and lovely face of Rām. "Blue" is the color of Rām and Krishna, the color in which they are always depicted in wall and scroll paintings in Bihar and elsewhere. "Elephant pearls" are the "pearls" obtained from an elephant's temples.

"The sun god goes from view" because he is eclipsed by Rām's radiance. The fate of Sītā's father, King Janak, is grand because he has become the father-in-law of Rām.

SONG OF MARRIED JOY
SOHĀG

Sohāg songs are sung when the bridegroom puts the vermilion mark on the bride's forehead under the wedding canopy. *Sohāg* is
the joyful state of being a wife.

93

Of what is the basket
Of what is the vessel
Oh where are you going?
Oh where are you going?
Whose daughter asks for the red mark?
Of gold is the basket
Of silver is the vessel
Oh where are you going?
Oh where are you going?
Whose daughter asks for the red mark?
To the hamlet of Mahādeo I am going,
O Gaurī, your red mark
Gaurī, your red mark
Give me the red mark I want.
I will give to all
Red powder in little parcels of leaves,
But for this daughter, this daughter
I will fill her lap.

The red mark is the mark of the married state and in asking for it
from Gaurī (the wife of Mahādeo or Shiva), the girl is asking for it
from the perfect wife. The implication is that such a mark will bring
with it a lifetime of married happiness.

OBSTRUCTION SONGS
ROKĀ

"Obstruction" songs are sung at the worship of the door, soon after the bridegroom's party has reached the bride's village; and again when the bridegroom is conducted to the bridal chamber once the wedding is over. At the door worship, the two parties compete with each other in singing *rokā* and *gajal*, and at the door of the chamber the bridegroom is obstructed until he has recited a satisfactory *gajal*, a witty song of love.

94

With the bridegroom who came from afar
The girls are laughing and talking,
"I won't let you into the chamber
I won't let you touch the bride,
Till you sing us a song
I won't let you in,
And your sister who's with you
Till you get her to dance
I won't let you in."

"To the father who came a long way
Give a good feast,
My father left my mother at home
Send your mother to him.
Give me my present and let me go."

The girls laugh and reply,
"You were shy in bringing your mother

But you didn't feel shy with your sister,
First put your sister with my brother
And then go into the chamber.
Such a bridegroom
I won't let into the chamber."

95

Bismila Rahmani Rahim
Listen to my song
The party has come to the bride's door
And it camps in the garden,
The coaches are drawn by elephants and horses
There are tents and screens
The bridegroom alights
The father stays in the litter,
They are weary from the long journey.
Listen, O daughter of my father-in-law,
You are my little sister,
Do not keep me any longer from the bride,
There are two little things under her slips
Red is the sign on her head
You are my life.

96

O Ladies,
With your sweet bodies
And your lovely walk
Hear what I recite.
With the help of your eyes
Admit me to the chamber
Come, O bride of my bed,
Come, O darling love of my heart,
And listen to my songs.

97

O little sisters,
Hear what I say
Why do you stop me?
Hear just one word
Why do you stop me?
Listen, O women of the house,
My words have no sting,
Why do you stop me?
In the end I shall enter the room
Dried fruits and betel I shall eat
And I shall not feel shy,
Why do you stop me?
Give me now the promised gift.

The little sisters to whom this song is addressed are the younger sisters of the bride.

98

I'll give the bridegroom a watch and chain
But I won't let him into the chamber,
That little bastard I won't let him in
Till he sings me a song I won't let him in
Till he sings me a love-song I won't let him in.
Till he gets his sister to dance
I won't let him in,
I'll stay on hour after hour
Till he gets her to dance
I won't let him in.
The smiling girls stop the bridegroom
Saying "Such a groom we won't let in."
Shy is the bridegroom and he says nothing.
"Give your grandmother to my grandfather

Give your mother to my father
Give your sister to my brother."
Such a young stranger I won't let in
Such a young bridegroom I won't let in.

BLESSING THE GROOM
PARICHHAN

Parichhan songs are sung when the bridegroom's mother and the other women are brandishing the curry-roller over his head and circling him with balls of cow dung. This is done just prior to his departure for the bride's house and again at the door of the bridal chamber.

99

O mother-in-law, bless the lovely groom
Your eyes will be soothed
And your heart will swell with gladness,
Take a gold plate, put lights on it
And the grains of rice
Wave it over the lovely groom.
O wife of the bride's brother
Your heart will swell with gladness
Your eyes will be soothed.

SONGS OF THE BRIDAL CHAMBER
KOHBAR

Kohbar songs are sung during the wedding period and when the bride
and bridegroom are conducted to the chamber.

100

I grind a plate of sandal
And mark the chamber
And there the bridegroom
Sleeps with the bride.
On his left he sleeps
And speaks no words
The bride's mother wakes him
And asks him why he's sad,
"Is the dowry too little
Is the wealth small?
Is the bride little
Why are you sad?"
"The dowry's not little
The wealth's not meager
The bride's not little
And I'm not at all sad.
Today no dog should bark
And no watchman go his rounds
Today I'll pick oranges and feed my wife.
Get up, little wife, and rinse your mouth
Rinse your mouth and eat an orange."

101

The wife of the bride's brother
Comes to paint the bridal chamber
Red paint in her hand
Betel juice in her mouth.
"O wife of the bride's brother,
Paint the chamber
So that it charms the eyes,
O wife of the bride's brother
On the walls of the chamber
Paint the ideal marriage
Between the bamboo and the lotuses,
In this room the bridegroom
Will sleep with his queen."
"Which is my mother-in-law?
Which is the wife of my bride's brother?
Which is my bride's sister?"
"The yellow shawl
And the yellow silk
She is my mother,
The red sari with a flowered edge
And the penciled eyes
She is the wife of my brother,
The one who came hurrying
And ran off after slapping me
She is my sister,
This chamber was painted
By my brother's wife
And she is my dearest."

SONGS FOR THE GROOM'S PARTY
JEWANĀR

Jewanār songs are sung by the women when the bridegroom's party is squatting at the bride's house for the wedding dinner.

102

The day Rām came to Janakpur
All the world went to see him,
One girl is standing another is sitting
A third shifts round to see him.
All of them wear pretty skirts
Their saris have golden fringes
Their oranges strain upwards
Like a lusty elephant's is their walk
Bells tinkle on their ankles.
On a bed in Janak's palace
Sit the four brothers,
The ladies peep through windows.
Wearing their yellow girdles
The brothers sit for their meals.
"Listen O Rām, to a story
And I'll sing you insults:

Three hundred and sixty
Are the mothers in your house,
But only three are queens.
Give one of these to Janak
And he'll give her every care

Rām's mother Kausalyā
He praises over much
Bharat's mother Kaikeyī
Indra longs to have."

"Oranges," as in song 53, refer to a girl's breasts. The comparison
of the girl's walk to the easy ambling gait of the elephant is a conven-
tion in Indian folk songs as well as in classical Indian poetry. In the
Vishnu Purana, when Krishna meets Kālindī she is described as a
beautiful girl "with a face like a moon, gazelle-eyed, with the voice
of a bird, and the gait of the elephant, with a waist slim as a lion-
ess."[62]

The girdle is a thin piece of cloth or several strands of thread,
tied round the waist of a young boy. When a boy is being rubbed
with oil, the oil trickles down, collects at the girdle, and slowly seeps
into the belly, in this way strengthening it.

103

In a gold plate the camphor burns
And they are swinging it round Krishna.
"How can I sing insults to Lāl?"
"Sing them you must
For insult is a form of love."
Today is lucky for a guest has come
And they welcome him at the palace
They put a gold bed in the court
They ask him to take off his clothes
Ganges water they bring in a gold jar
And Arjun washes his feet,
He washes his feet, he drinks the water
And says how lucky he is.
Sweets and sugared candies
A dish of butter

Dried fruits of every kind,
Fruits in plenty they bring
And Krishna sits to eat
And now the girls begin to tease him,
"How can you girls abuse me?
I am lord of the three worlds."
"If you are lord of the three worlds
Why have you come to your father-in-law's?"
"Abuse me as you like
I will hold out an apron."
"Jasodā is your mother
And men and sages praise her,
Kuntī-devī is your father's sister
And she had a child before she married,
Subadrā-rānī is your sister
And she ran off with Arjun,
Father Nand is your father
And he lives wrapped in a blanket,
You yourself dance with the milkmaids
What more shall I say?
O Krishna you have all these faults
And you call yourself lord of the three worlds?
Do not boast while I am here
Or I'll let out everything
Oh how can I sing insults to Krishna?"

The term for an abuse or an insult is *gālī*. At weddings, it is a
form of ritually bawdy song in suggestive language. *Gālī* songs almost
always have sexual themes and often they imply the ill repute of the
women of the groom's family. They are part of the general relaxation
of customary restraints which characterize a wedding.[63]

SONGS OF THE GROOM'S ANOINTMENT
ĀBTAUNI

Ābtauni songs are often sung when the bridegroom's body is being
rubbed with mustard or saffron prior to his starting on the return
journey home.

104

In a gold cup
I make the saffron paste
And rub it on the bridegroom's body
The Brahman utters prayers,
The women sing their joy.
The mother wipes his mouth with her sari
The father's sister pencils his eyes
The elder brother's wife fans his head,
The women sing their joy.
The father's brother's wife wipes his mouth
The elder sister pencils his eyes
The mother's brother's wife fans his head,
The women sing their joy.

105

Oil of mustard, oil of mustard
The bridegroom is rubbed with oil.
The mother whose husband is living
Rubs the oil;
Her bangles shake

Her eyes wander
The boy sits to be rubbed
The bridegroom is rubbed with oil.

106

On the mountain is the oil god,
O oilman press some mustard oil.
My grandfather grows mustard
My grandmother stores the oil
My bridegroom's body is thin
And cannot bear the smart.

INTERLUDES AND CODAS
JHŪMAR

Jhūmar songs are sung throughout the wedding period partly as interludes in the singing and partly as songs with which to end a night's ritual singing.

107

Why do you catch my wrist?
Two bangles if they're rare
Are enough for beauty
But ordinary bangles
Must fill the arm.
The lover touches her finger
The lover catches her wrist
The lover strokes her breast
Let me go or my name will be gone.

108

Powder your teeth, lovely one,
Powder your teeth and smile,
To your husband's house you must go.
Put slips on your breasts, lovely one,
Then loosen the slips and bare them,
Put on a skirt, lovely one,
Put it on and bend,
Make up a bed, lovely one,
Make it and bear his embrace,
To your husband's house you must go.

109

In a golden dish I set the food
But she powders her teeth and does not eat
That lovely girl
Powders her teeth in a mirror.
In a golden jar I brought Ganges water
But she powders her teeth and does not drink
That lovely girl
Powders her teeth in a mirror.

110

In a golden dish she placed the food
But he did not eat,
She weeps and weeps
And her eyes are red
"You should help me to eat, lovely one,
Now it is you I have to help."
She weeps and weeps
And her eyes are red.

111

Throughout the night he drives a car,
In a golden dish I set his food
"Eat it, you motor man, my darling,
In a golden jar is Ganges water
Drink it, you motor man, my darling."

112

Without a light I cannot go to bed.
"How lovely you look
With your red line and your pearls."
From Bhagalpur a whore comes

From Gorakhpur comes her lover.
Without a light I cannot go to bed.

113

As I clamber on the bed my anklets tinkle,
The mother-in-law and her daughter lurk about.
"Husband, do not pester me,
I am still a young girl,
O husband, do not pester me.
Wait patiently till my full youth comes
Then I'll bow at your feet and beg you,
But now my years are tender,
O husband, do not trouble me."

114

You must make a house
On the sand, O husband.
The house will look well
Only with a red bed,
The red bed will look well
Only when two are on it,
The two will look well
Only with a baby in their arms,
The child will look well
When his hair is cut at Banaras,
The hair-cutting will look well
Only when your younger sister is there,
Your younger sister will look well
When there is money in your waist.
Make a house on the sand,
My absent husband.

115

Who threw a ball at the sun?
The landlord's daughter cooked food
And a thousand kings come to feast
Who threw a ball at the sun?

116

"O wife, if someone catches your wrist
And takes you off what will you do?"
"I'll go to the police station
And tell the Sub-inspector,
I'll tell the Inspector."
"O wife, what will you do?"
"I'll go to the outpost
And tell the constable,
I'll tell the Head Constable."
"O wife what will you do?"
"I'll go to the court
And tell the Collector,
I shall tell the District Magistrate."

117

"Throw a rope and scale the wall, my darling."
To the door comes the lover
But the dog of the house barks.
He enters the court
But the scorpion of the house stings him.
"Throw a rope and scale the wall, my darling."
He lies in bed and the house ants bite him.
"Throw a rope and scale the wall, my darling."

118

Calcutta town has a bad name
But the eyes cannot resist it,
To his mother he sends a letter
To his wife his kind regards.
Calcutta town has a bad name
To his mother he sends five rupees
To his wife a full fifty.
The eyes cannot resist it,
Oh a bad name has Calcutta town.

In the poem, the demoralizing effect of Calcutta is seen in the
slight to the mother, for in a Kayasth family, the wife can never be
as important as the mother or rank as high. In India as in England
there is a tendency for the country to regard the town as wicked,
and in Bihar a trip to Calcutta is regarded much as a trip to Paris is
regarded in England.

TAPĀ

A *tapā* is comparable to a *jhūmar* and is sung at the same times.

119

"The *champa* is in bud
But still my darling I will pick it
I could not pick the *champa* bud
And my shawl was torn, my darling.
To the tailor's shop I went at once
O darling, sew my shawl."
"Why should I sew your shawl?"
"O darling, come into my bed."
"Why should I come into your bed?"

The *champa* (*Michelia Champaca*) in bud is an image for the girl's breasts and the girl is also the tailor.

120

Do not catch me so
Very small is my waist,
You hold my finger
You hold my waist
And when you catch my breasts
My life almost goes.

121

Grand is the bridge of Banaras
Where sits an old woman

And an old man flirts.
Grand is the bridge of Banaras
Where sits a young woman
And the gangster flirts.
Grand is the bridge of Banaras
Where sits a girl
And the boys make love.
Grand is the bridge of Banaras
Where squats the pretty whore
And the gangster eyes her.

SONGS OF CHILDBEARING
AND LOVE

SONGS OF LOVE
DOHĀ

Among certain Indian castes and tribes, the short poem of two lines is a common form of love poem. The Baigas, for instance, use the *dadaria,* a simple two- to four-line verse form, when they are flirting in the jungle. Compare the following two poems:

> I have put a bullet in my new gun
> Come on, my bed, I will put a new girl on you.

> The stalk of the creeper is twining upwards
> The girl I've just enjoyed is sitting by my side.[64]

The Pathans, also, use "an unconnected series of two-lined pieces known as *'tappā'* or *'misrā,'* which usually have a love content." The following are two examples.

Three things in a girl are pleasing to the sight;
The golden amulet on her neck, her fair calves, her delicate walk.

I belong to Swat and live here in the plains with my lover
May Allah destroy the plains, so that both of us may go and live in Swat.[65]

Among the Bhojpuri Kayasths, the *dohā,* a couplet or short poem of varying rhythms, is a form anonymously composed and circulated through the villages by oral repetition. These are introduced into the letters which a newly married couple exchange when the boy is parted from the girl, and they serve the function of amorous ornaments.

Letter-writing usually occurs when the boy is forced to leave the village after his marriage in order to go on with his studies. If he is attracted to his wife, he will try to write to her and she in turn will try to write back. This writing of letters is not, however, regarded by Kayasth society as a charming proof of fidelity but rather as a thing for censure. It is inferred that the boy is wife-mad and will not attend to his books and, far from being encouraged, it is frowned upon. Any correspondence that goes on has therefore to be semi-secret, to be written in private and to be posted through servants. In the case of the girl, surrounded by her husband's family, to send a letter is hard but to get a letter is even harder. And it is, on the whole, husbands who get letters from their wives rather than wives from their husbands. If a husband sends a letter, it becomes general talk in the family that he is writing to his wife and sooner or later one of his uncles drops him a hint that he had better stop it.

In their tone and elegant artificiality, certain *dohās* are not unlike minor Elizabethan lyrics or even valentines.

122

The eyes long to see you
The arms ache to hold you
Without you the body cannot move
And the limbs are weak,
My life is happy in your love
And the ears thrill at your talk
I say your name and my passion is calmed
But the eyes droop from not seeing you.

123

My lover, you loved me
And tore out my heart,
I cannot rest unless I see you
O hear me,
You sweet thief.

124

The bee is mad without its honey
The cuckoo is mad without spring
And you being absent I am like them,
May God be my witness!

In almost all Indian popular poetry, the bee is associated with love
and the lover, as in the Bengali ballad of Kamala: "Youth has dawned
on you, fair damsel, but you live the stern life of a nun. When the
flower blooms, the bees gather, but no bee visits a withered
flower. . . . Many are the bees that have been maddened by you,
my adored flower! Why do you keep yourself concealed from them?"[66]
Bees also appear in the Pathan poem:

O thine eyes are like the bees, in the garden of the world,[67]
Making honey out of the blossoms of love.

———————

125

Darling with what delight I sip
The poison of your love,
Only the nectar of absence saves me
And I live to die.

126

Darling I tried a million times to see you
Why does God keep us apart?

127

How to reprove God for giving us two bodies?
Why did he not give one to my lover and me?

128

Having caught me in your net of love,
Why have you grown cold
And left me here to mourn your going?

129

At my frenzy thousands of mountains
Have turned to water,
But your heart has not melted, my murderer,
Your heart is harder than a stone.

130

Do not fall in love but if you do
Do not make it and then break it,
Breaking, you must mend it
And the knot has no beauty.

131

In me is nothing mine
In me are all things yours,
I give you what is yours
And do not lose what's mine.

132

Whom shall I tell: What shall I say?
Struck with love's arrow
It is the eyes' mischief and pain.

133

Love does not grow in a garden
Love is not sold in a market,

Whoever wants it, subject or king
May walk with it on his head.

134

To him who knows not love
No use explaining,
Frogs live in water
They do not mix with fish.

135

The poet weeps when God calls him
The joy of a lover's presence is not in heaven.

136

When a lover is in the market
The market is a desert,
Find him in a desert
And the desert is a market.

GAJAL

Gajal songs are either about love affairs or sexual troubles, and are sung for amusement any time in the year. Many of them contain Urdu words and are possibly of Muhammadan origin. They are sung by Kayasths as part of their reservoir of village poetry.

137

A husband must not be small, O friend,
A husband must not be small.
A little husband who was sent for water
Came back home with a broken pot,
    Oh that little husband.
A little husband who was sent for *gānjā*
Came back home with a broken pipe,
    Oh that little husband.
A little husband who was sent to court
Came back home with the papers torn,
Came back home with a broken pen,
    Oh that little husband.
O Mother Gangā and Mother Sarjū
Gather and bear off little boys,
Pebbles and stones have all been drowned
Gather and bear off little boys,
    Oh that little husband.

Usually the girl is younger than the boy but it sometimes happens that the boy is younger than the girl. This occurs when the girl's

parents fail to make a suitable match and in despair are forced to
marry her to anyone whose parents will agree.

138

Such a silly husband I have
He has forgotten to hold hands
To plant a garden
And plant a grove
He has forgotten
To plant lemon trees,
He has forgotten
To build a house with two stories
And to make a room,
He has forgotten
To make windows
He has forgotten
To make a bed
And cover it with a white sheet,
He has even forgotten
To sleep with his other wife.

139

On my neck he put a gold necklace
And away he crept, oh where has he gone?
In a golden cage twitters a partridge,
Help me to hear what the partridge says.
The ring is of gold
And the stone is green
This is the mark
On a lover's mind.

The meaning is that the husband has tamed a partridge who acts
as his proxy. The husband goes away but the bird remains. Since

the wife cannot talk to the husband, she listens to the partridge. But
the husband still wears the ring and perhaps he will return.

140

"Darling, I am giving myself to you,
Let go of the cloth on my breasts."
"I will let it go
On the road where the motors pass,
I will let it go
On the railway line,
I will let it go
At the well where the women gather,
I will let it go
In the garden where the flowers are planted,
I will let it go
On the bed of your darling
Where lovers have their sport."

In this poem the husband or lover is catching hold of the woman's
anchara, the end part of her sari, and pulling her towards the bed.
The woman is making a mock show of resistance.

141

Darling in the shade of my nose-ring
You pass the noon.
Four months lasts the heat,
Sweat trickles from my lips
And you wave a pretty fan above me.
Four months the rain falls
Drip drop drip drop
Make me a house of love.
Four months lasts the cold
And how the heart shivers
Put your arm round my neck.

A *jhūlanī* is a small nose-ring put between the two nostrils and dangling over the upper lip.

142

That lovely girl is out to make trouble
And soon will my heart be ruled with care,
Soon shall I share a secret with her.
Do not walk like a flirt,
Mincing at every step
Watching you walk is the death of the world,
Sometimes you say yes and sometimes no
And only for a kiss we bicker.

143

Darling open your body
And if I look, what of it?
Let me hear your pretty voice
If I hear, what of it?
Give me a dish of love
And if I eat
What of it?

144

If you show me your face like a moon
What of it?
My heart burns with love
If you quench my burning heart
What of it?
I scorned my heart
And went mad for you,
If you let me smell the scent
Of your cheeks like a flower
What of it?

Bismil says
How my heart longs to meet you,
If only you would come
And mix your heart with mine
Would it do us any harm?

The comparison of the face to the moon is a standard device in popular Indian poetry. Compare, for example, the Bengali ballad of Dewan Bhatna.

As soon as the Dewan heard the report of her arrival, he hastened to meet her in the boat. He was maddened with her beauty; it seemed to him that the full moon had fallen down from the sky to his city.[68]

BIRTH SONGS
SOHAR

In village households, the desire of the man and the wife is for a son—partly for carrying on the family and partly so that the funeral ritual may be done correctly at the man's death. There is no question of postponing children, and a couple tries to have a child as soon as the girl can bear one.

145

A house of two stories King Dasrath has made
But without a balcony I do not like it,
A tank King Dasrath has dug
But without a temple I do not like it,
A grove King Dasrath has planted
But without a cuckoo I do not like it,
A bed King Dasrath has made
But without a son I do not like it.

King Dasrath is here used as a term for the husband. A balcony is needed so that the women may come and sit by it and look down on the street; a temple, because after bathing in a tank it is proper to go and say prayers; and a cuckoo because without its loud and lively song the grove will be gloomy.

146

I am slim as a betel leaf
And lovely as a flower,
My husband goes to Madhuban

And flirts with the flower-girl.
Join me, my friends,
Come in a crowd to Madhuban
And look at my husband's temple.
To one wood they go
To another they go
In the third wood, O little one,
They see the husband's temple
Where he flirts with the flower-girl.
"O flower-girl, with your wiles
How did you enchant the king
And what delight do you give him?"
"O lovely lady,
I spread betel leaves and scatter blossoms
I fan him the whole night
And I bewitch him with my eyes."

In the poems, the flower-girl is a slightly sinister figure. She minis-
ters to a need—the blossom at the wedding and the bridegroom's
marriage crown—but her name is always unpleasant in a bride's ear
and suggests a furtive infidelity. She is comparable to the flower-girl
in Rowlandson's drawings and the recognition by the upper classes
in England that the vulgarity of lower-class women often marks a
greater sexual power.

There is a parallel situation in Morocco. "When a youth is betrothed, some negresses whose profession is to assist women on fes-
tive occasions dress him up as a bride with garments which they
brought with them. . . . One of the negresses gives him some milk
to drink which is supposed to make his life 'white,' and another puts
into his mouth a date representing wealth."[69] The negress as a men-
acing stranger corresponds to the flower-girl with her dangerous charm.

Madhuban is a garden near Brindaban where Krishna went and
forgot the milkmaids. To go to Madhuban, therefore, is to go away
and forget one's loyalties. "Temple" is used because, to a wife, any

place where her husband stays is a temple. Betel leaves are very soft
and smooth and therefore make a pleasant couch.

When a girl ceases to menstruate, she ceases to observe the men-
struation taboos[70] and it is this which causes her condition to leak
out in the family. Her mother-in-law usually questions her and then
takes precautions against her eating anything bad or doing any heavy
work. From the second month particular care is taken against evil
spirits.[71] The girl is kept inside at night and not allowed to sit in the
courtyard alone.

147

First I bow to Ganesh and then to all the gods,
O little one,
When I conceive a son, I will sing for joy.
As the second month passes
Fits of sickness come
O little one,
Betel no longer charms
And only sleep brings ease.
When the third month comes
I tell the mother-in-law
I can cook no longer.
For my little joy is troubling me.
As the fourth month passes
The *nanad* smiles and says
O little one,
I shall take the bangle from your wrist
For dangling your baby boy.
When the fifth month passes
She tells her husband
O little one,
I will not sleep on the low bed
And you must sit and fan me.

When the sixth month passes
The mother-in-law
Marks how the first step falls
And tells if it will be a boy.
As the seventh month passes
She tells her husband,
I cannot bear the heat
You must sit and fan me.
When the eighth month passes
The eight parts grow heavy
O little one,
The sari is always slipping from the waist
And I am always retying it.
As the ninth month passes
The *nanad* smiles and says,
O little one,
Tell me when your boy comes
And I will give away pearls.
When the tenth month passes
O little one,
A child is born
In the house of King Dasrath
And songs of joy are heard.

When a girl becomes pregnant, her *nanad* (husband's younger sister) gives her notice that she will demand a particular gift for doing a special rite on the sixth day after the birth. If the girl agrees, all is well; but often she says she cannot part with the thing the *nanad* has named and then a quarrel ensues. The neighbors come flocking in and only after a voluble scene is the matter finally settled. The gift a *nanad* asks is usually one of the ornaments which the girl is wearing, or if she is not keen on an ornament, she demands a present of money—five, ten, or fifty rupees according to the girl's means. If the *nanad* is unmarried, her wishes have no special importance as the family can humor her in other ways. But once she is married, it means that her connection with the family is cut. She no longer gets her food and clothes from her father, the scope for her wishes is narrow and it is all the more important that her whims should be granted. To refuse an unmarried *nanad* is difficult but not serious; to refuse a married *nanad* is of major importance for the whole balance of family life is involved.

"The falling of the first step" relates to the mother-in-law noticing the foot on which her daughter-in-law starts walking. The two may be talking in the courtyard and the daughter-in-law turns to go in. The leg she puts out first is the leg noted by the mother-in-law. If it is the left leg, the baby will be a girl; if it is the right leg, the baby will be a boy. Throughout the month, the mother-in-law will be on the alert, noticing her movements and taking a census of the signs.

148

Eight years old I was
And at nine was my *gaunā*,
Twelve years old I was
And to a strange land my husband went.
He told me to make a tall house
And roof it with tiles
To get a baby in my lap
And then he would come.
She hears his words
And stands in the courtyard
And her younger *dewar*
Comes from outside,
"Why is my *bhaujī* sad?"
"O *dewar*, my *dewar*
Listen to my plight,
O *dewar*, heavy is the task
Your brother has given me

And I have no heart.
He told me to make a tall house
And roof it with tiles
To get a baby in my lap
And then he would come."
"O *bhaujī*, my *bhaujī*,
You good girl,
Dress up like a whore
And go to my brother
Stay with him eight days
Then say you are going.
Tell him you spurn his sixty gold coins
But make him part with his ring."
For eight days stays the *bhaujī*
And on the ninth she is going,
She spurns the sixty gold coins
And takes his ring.
A crowd gathers
And the brother says
"What a silly little whore
To want only a ring."
Gone are twelve years
And he's standing in the courtyard.
"Tell me whose baby
Romps in your lap?"
She takes off the ring
And she throws it on the ground.
"See your own ring
And blame me if you can."

The *gaunā* is the second marriage—the ceremony after which the bride goes and lives with the bridegroom. Verrier Elwin in *The Baiga* has shown how very early sexual intercourse begins among Baiga boys and girls although pregnancy does not result until a much later age,

say seventeen or eighteen. Nine, although a very abnormal age among
Kayasths, is not, therefore, an impossible age for a little girl to start
living with her husband.

The *dewar* is the husband's younger brother—the only male in the
house with whom the young bride is allowed to talk on easy terms
and in whom she can confide. Compare the Baiga poem

> How hard it is to live here!
> My *māmī*[72] hits me with her fists,
> My *nanad* tweaks my cheeks
> Only one there is who keeps me happy
> And that is my handsome young *dewar*.[73]

As in poem 111, the theme is again the theme of the unfaithful
husband, the fear that, while the wife is impure and therefore away
from her husband, he will go and amuse himself with another girl.
In the poem the twelve years are not so much twelve years as the
twelve days of separation, the meaning being that the days pass so
heavily that it is as if they were years.

When a woman feels her pains starting, she first tells her *nanad*
(husband's younger sister), and if there is no *nanad* in the house she
tells her mother-in-law. The *nanad* is told because of her ritual position as the *dewar's* sister—the person with whom her talk may be
candid and for whom the husband's exclusive claims are relaxed. As
soon as the *nanad* and mother-in-law learn her condition, they empty
the living room. Some fire is damped down in a pot so that it gives
out only smoke and the pot is then placed in the doorway. A string
bed and a stool are put in the room, and the woman is dressed in an
old and torn sari. She strips herself of ornaments.[74] The locks in all
the boxes are unlocked and she unties her hair.[75] She then squats
on the stool or lies on the bed and covers herself with a thin sheet.

As the pains grow, the women of the house rub her with mustard
oil and give her hot water and hot milk and butter to drink. At last
the child is born, but it is not at first moved. Instead, the women

take a little water and spit on its mouth. Then when the afterbirth
has come out it is shifted away from its mother and kept apart until
the midwife comes.

For calling the midwife a set procedure is observed. A male member of the family is sent hurrying out with a knife or sickle in his
hand[76] and a seer of rice or barley. He gives the rice to the midwife
as a present, tells her a baby has been born and then starts back
with her. When the midwife reaches the house, she purifies herself
by washing her hands and feet and sprinkling water on her head.
She then drives away any evil spirit that may be on her by shaking
out her sari and touching the fire at the door of the bedroom. She
then enters and gets to work on the baby.

She first rubs it with mustard oil, dusts it with wheat powder, and
removes any mucus with a towel. She then knots the cord with some
thread and cuts the cord above the knot with a sickle. After that the
baby is bathed and dried.

The midwife then makes the mother stand up and rubs her head
against her belly.[77] She then changes the mother's sari, puts some
rice in her hands, does the blessing gestures over her, and finally,
after tossing the baby up, she puts it in the mother's lap. As she does
so, the father's sister strikes a bell-metal bowl with a small stick and
the women sing songs praising Mātā or Devī and invoking the ancestors.

The barber's wife is then sent out to call in the neighbors, and as
they swarm in they are given oil and vermilion powder for their heads.
Sohar or birth songs are sung in chorus—and the noise of the singing
fills the house. When the singing is over and the women have gone,
one of the men wards off all evil spirits by planting a thorny branch
in the doorway.[78]

A day or two later, a Brahman is called to prepare the child's horoscope. A dish containing rice, *dūb* grass, a rupee, and some turmeric
is set before him, and after consulting an almanac he writes out the
horoscope and fixes a date for the nail-paring ceremony. He also de-
cides the day for the mother to take her first bath.

On the sixth day, when the mother becomes pure, the neighbors are again invited. A band is summoned, and the mother comes out of the bedroom with a sickle in her hand. She is rubbed with mustard oil and then along with the baby she is washed in water which has been boiled with *nīm* leaves.[79] As this goes on, the neighbors sing *sohar* songs. Oil and vermilion powder are then presented to them, and the mother retires once more to the birth chamber. The effect of this ceremony is to make her partly pure. On the twelfth day after the delivery she is completely pure[80] and returns to ordinary life. The form called "Shiva Mai," resembling an elephant with a rider, is outlined on a wall of the confinement room and *pūjā* is done by putting butter and vermilion powder on it. The mother's feet are then colored with henna, her nails are cut, and her body is washed. A feast follows, and with this act of gaiety she returns to normal life.

149

From Calcutta comes my husband
From Darbhanga he comes,
O little one,
And he brings a pretty sari
To please his darling.
From the back of the house
She calls a carpenter,
O little one.
"Make a narrow bed
For us both to sleep on."
On one side she's sleeping
The lovely wife
On the other he's sleeping
The handsome young traveler,
He puts out his arm
And she gets in a temper,
O little one.

In her mouth he puts betel
And sprays her with roses,
O little one.
He smiles and puts his arm round her neck
And the lovely wife is happy,
She has written a letter
To the handsome young traveler,
O little one.
"Today is the boy's sixth day
And home you must come.
Where shall I get cloth?
Where shall I get a tailor?
O little one."
"Measure his size and make a shirt
And I'll put it on my baby.
Where shall I get gold?
Where shall I get a goldsmith?
O little one."
"I'll get some ringing bells.
And stitch them on the shirt
Tumuki tumuki the little one will go
And I and my husband will watch him."

When a husband comes home after being away, he usually brings his wife a silk sari or a bodice, but if his parents are alive, he has to smuggle it in so that the gift may not seem a slight to his mother. To demonstrate any love for his wife is seemingly to prefer her to his mother and this is improper and incorrect, a gesture that strikes at the basis of joint family life. If he loves his wife, therefore, a husband always brings her a present but at the same time he always keeps it secret that he has done so.

In the poem, the situation is that the husband comes home, sleeps with his wife, again goes away and is called back to attend the *chhathi* ceremony of his son. This occurs on the sixth or twelfth day after

the delivery when the baby is dressed up in a new shirt and is given
bells or bangles. The wife calls her husband home because unless he
gives her money the clothes and bells will not be bought.

150

From the milk of a magic cow
She made a rice-pudding,
O little one,
But the husband is angry
The king is angry
And he treats it as poison.
"O neighbors, you are my
Husband's sisters
Tell me what to do
That I may see my husband
That I may see my king."
"On your head put a basket
In your hand take a broom
In the guise of a sweeper
Go and gaze at your king,
First sweep the elephant shed
Then sweep the stables
Then sweep the room where the king sits
And gaze at your king,
Gaze at your husband."
She puts a basket under her arm
In her hand she takes a broom
In the guise of a sweeper
She goes to see her king,
She goes to see her husband.
First she sweeps the elephant's shed
Then she sweeps the stables,
Then she sweeps the king's room.

Smiling is her king
Smiling is her husband.
"O king, you're lord of the realm
And I'm only a sweeper
Why do you laugh at me?"
"The knot of your sari is smart,
Neat is the parting of your hair
Like a split pulse,
As lovely as Rādhā Rukminī's
Is your little waist, O sweeper."

In this poem, the husband is the king and the king is the husband. The neighbors are called "sisters-in-law" because a wife consults her sisters-in-law whenever she is worried. She disguises herself as a sweeper, for a sweeper goes anywhere and everywhere and would not be noticed or commented on.

151

Slim is that fair-skinned girl
Who sobs against the door,
"O little one,
Sharp are my pains
And no one is stirring."
Up gets the father's maid
And lights a lamp.
"Your fault it was, O darling
Not to have called me,
If you had woken me
I could have called my mother,
If you had woken me
I could have called my sister."
"O my husband, when a girl is in pain
She alone can bear it—
Stand ready to play with the baby."

In this song the getting-up of the husband is understood. The father's maid lights a lamp and it is the husband who then speaks.

152

"O tailor's son
Look to your dress
O son of the groom
Look to your horse
O wife
Tie the bells on my stockings
As I start for a far land."
"When I was young and innocent
You did not go to a far land
Now I am with child, O king,
To a far land you go."

"O wife, your words calm me
Tell me what you fancy."
"I care for nothing in the house,
Get me only some minnows."
I cast the net once
And again I cast the net
And a third time I cast the net
And caught the minnows for my queen.
The girl is sleeping,
He goes and wakes her
And sits her on his knee.
"Rinse your mouth from the jar
And come and eat some fish."
"Take the fish away
Take the fish away
I do not want it,
I die from the pain in my side,
O king, call a nurse."

> Half the night goes
> And in the second half
> A boy is born
> The music starts from the bands
> And in the palace birth songs rise.

Just as the Duchess of Malfi craved for apricots, pregnant women are susceptible to curious cravings. Kayasth women are reported to have an overwhelming desire to eat yellow earth, to chew tiles, to swallow some parched rice or gram, or to eat raw fish.

RITES OF TONSURE
MUNDAN

At times of difficult delivery, the mother and grandmother vow that if the child is born safely and is a son, they will do the tonsure ceremony. This ceremony takes place either at the Ganges or in a temple to Shiva or Devī, and is usually done when the child is five years old.

When the rites are performed at the Ganges, incense is burnt, the boy is placed in his mother's lap, the barber comes and puts down a little dish of water, and the women then circle around, passing two anna bits over the boy's head and tossing them into the barber's dish. The barber then shaves the boy's head with a razor and the hair is gathered in the sari of the grandmother or an aunt. When the hair cutting is over, the grandmother bows before the Ganges and prays that as the boy's hair has been offered, so he may be blessed. She then casts the hair on the water.

A ceremony known as "the garlanding of the Ganges" then follows. A peg is put in the ground and to it is tied an enormous ball of string decorated with mango leaves and marigold flowers. The string is then taken across the river in a boat. Incense is offered and the string is allowed to drift away on the current.

When the rites are performed at a temple, the garlanding is omitted, Shiva or Devī are asked to bless the boy, and the hair is then shaken out on the ground, to be dispersed by the wind.

The following relatives are usually invited to the ceremony: the boy's aunts (father's sisters), his great aunts (his grandfather's sisters) his uncle (his mother's brother), and besides these, any close friends of the family. Wherever possible, the invitations are carried

by a barber, but if the relatives live far away and the Kayasth father
cannot afford to send the barber, he writes a letter. But within the
village and its neighborhood, to send the barber is mandatory.

The songs are sung while the arrangements are being made and
not during the actual worship.

153

Five are the leaves of betel
And they are pierced with a clove,
O Barber, go from house to house
And ask them all to come
For the tonsure of my son.
Call all the kinsmen
For the tonsure of my son,
Call the god of Gaya
Call the god of Prayag
For the tonsure of my son,
Call the god of Kashi
For the tonsure of my son.

154

"O my lord, my king,
Attend to what I say
Twelve years old is the boy
And you must cut his hair."
"O wife,
Think on what I say,
We'll need wheat and butter and sugar
For feeding the priests,
The sacred texts and a dhoti
And a pearl for the knot."

155

In the courtyard the father's sister stands
And calls to the rain god,
"God, do not thunder
God, do not let it shower
God, do not let the rain pour.
Today is my nephew's tonsure
And I will bless his fallen hair."

156

"Grandfather,
Hold an umbrella over his head
Grandmother,
Cover his head with your sari—
Today is the tonsure of the boy.
Hold the cut hair in your sari
And give him your blessing."
"Bless him I will, bless him I will
And I'll show it to all who have come,
Five pieces of gold and a sari
I shall carry as my present."

SONGS TO THE GODDESS
CHAITĀ

Chaitā songs are sung for fifteen days following the Holi festival, during the fast which is observed in honor of Devī, the goddess. The festival is a fertility one designed to ensure favorable sowing and germination, and for this reason it is associated with sexuality.

157

Friends comb their long hair
On the bank of the Jumna,
They comb their hair and bind it,
They put on red pearls.
Friends are combing their long hair
On the bank of the Jumna,
On the bank of the Jumna
Krishna is lurking
To beg a young breast.
Rādhā takes her garland
And puts it on Krishna.

MĀTĀ

This is another form of song associated with the period following Holi.

158

Lucky is today
For into our courtyard
Comes the mother goddess.
I will wash the courtyard
With a paste of sandal
And the goddess will come
With jingling feet,
In the courtyard she dances and sings.
What is her cot made of
And what are its four legs?
Her cot is of gold
And the legs are of silver.

SONGS OF THE RAINY SEASON
CHAUMĀSA

In the Waste Land, T. S. Eliot writes

> April is the cruelest month, breeding
> Lilacs out of the dead land, mixing
> Memory and desire, stirring
> Dull roots with spring rain.

But in India it is Sāwan or August which mixes memory and desire and drives lonely women frantic; and in almost all poems of the rains—*chaumāsa, kajalī* and *barsātī*—the theme is one of sexual frenzy.

There are two reasons for this intimate association. In the first place, the general gloom of the season turns loneliness into an active fear and intensifies the need of a wife for her husband. And, secondly, the imagery of the season itself evokes sexual longing.

In early Chinese poetry, clouds were often images for multitudes:

> Outside the Eastern Gate
> Are girls many as the clouds;
> But though they are many as clouds
> There is none on whom my heart dwells.
> White jacket and grey-scarf
> Alone could cure my woe.[81]

> In the wicker fish-trap by the bridge
> Are fish, both bream and roach.
> A lady of Ch'i goes to be married;
> Her escort is like a trail of clouds.[82]

But in Indian poetry, clouds have a drifting instability.

> You are like a cloud
> That wanders in the sky.
> If you really loved me
> You would sleep close beside my heart.[83]

It is the waywardness of clouds rather than their number or ordered progression which haunts a woman in the rains, and fills her with tormenting thoughts of her husband.

Finally, there is rain itself. This occurs in poem 159 and its symbolism is latent in all poetry that springs from the rainy season.

> In the Urai jungle,
> Rain pours down in torrents
> If you would enjoy yourself,
> Do so before you're married.[84]

> The rain is pouring down,
> The lotus blooms on the water.
> There is a dark mango tree,
> The rain is pouring down.[85]

Because the falling rain evokes the act of love, the rains are a period of sexual strain.

The following *chaumāsa* poetry covers the six months of the rainy season and was collected in the Patna district of Bihar.[86]

159
ASAR

> Asar is the month of parting, friend
> The sky glowers with gloom
> Leaping and reeling the god rains
> And my sweet budding breasts are wet.

All my friends sleep with their husbands
But my own husband is a cloud in another land,
The whole night I sob
And cannot get still,
The fish shine in the river
The sword shines in the hand
The husband dazzles on the bed
And I long to fold myself round him.
In the black clouds the lightning shimmers,
How heavily it weighs
This parting from my husband.
I care for nothing in his absence
I fold my hands and I pray,
O God who made the world,
Listen to my prayer.

160

SĀWAN

Sāwan and the eager river leaps
The water streams
The paths vanish
Swamped are fields and threshing floors,
In the bushes insects murmur
And I tremble at the sound.
Happy is that woman's lot
Whose husband is at home,
Wretched is my fate
Whose husband has gone away.
Absence with its flame
Tortures me each day
And my lotus heart is on fire,
My husband tricked me
And ran to another land.

He cares for me no more.
And his heart is hard,
how my breasts tingle
And burst at their slips!

161

BHĀDO

Bhādo and with my husband
I am fast asleep on the bed,
Of a sudden on my wrist he pounces
And tastes the savor of my lips.
His syrup drips on the bed
Staining my petticoat,
Torn are my silk slips
Broken my pearl necklace
Sprained my frail wrists
But I feel no pain.
I lose my nose-ring and my jeweled pin
And as he struggles with me
I sweat the whole night.
All the fondling of my father's house
He has turned to dust,
All my sixteen points
My husband has spoiled.

162

ĀSIN

Āsin raised my hopes
I worshiped the sun night and day
But my husband never came from the strange land.
I am weary with longing
I collect buds and adorn my bed
And make myself smart in the sixteen ways,

But my smartness counts for nothing.
My hopes are shattered
Hard is the heart of my darling, O friend,
He sends me not a word.
With my husband far from me
I moan on my bed,
When the hawk cuckoo complains
Absence burns me,
When I fancy I hear my husband
My breast breaks and I am filled with fire.
Oh the torment of a husband in another land
And the torment of hearing the bird's cry.

163
KĀRTIK

Kārtik wakes the passions
And lack of love burns me all night,
I get no rest
I sob hour after hour
Morning comes weeping weeping.
A mere seven years is my husband
And my own age is twenty-four,
My husband is a little silly
Who does not know what to do.
Lying on my bed at night
Sleep never comes to my eyes
Beyond all bearing is my lack of love.
Madan is wearing me out,
The naughty fellow and my naughty breasts
Burst at their ribbons
My body tingles
And despite myself rapture comes.

164

AGHAN

Pleasant is Aghan. The fair lady
Sees the paddy all around
And writes to her lord.
My husband left me
And went to another land
And he cares for me no more.
I was only twelve years old
When he claimed and brought me here,
Now in my full bloom
When I am like a pomegranate
My husband is a cloud in another land.
Now when the lemons and oranges are ready
My husband shuns me.
The garden is in bloom my heartless love,
And in it the bee hovers—
Can't your heart see
That the garden withers for want of you?

SONGS OF AMUSEMENT
KAJALĪ

Kajalī poems are sung for amusement in the rains, either at noon or in the evening but not before midday. *Barsātī* is another name for *kajalī* and differs only in having a more frequent emphasis on the season.

165

How your face charms me, my darling
With a parting of pearls
Like snakes your curled hair
And your eyes with red lids, my darling.
If you strike only once with your eyes' dagger
You work a witch's wonder,
With your colored dress and your flowered slips
And your swaying walk
How your face charms me, my darling.

166

I have fallen in love
After glancing at you, my darling
With the arching curve on your brows
And your eyes' sign.
Madly I loiter in the market, my darling,
And in frenzy I see your breasts like oranges,
Your walk is a dance, my darling.
Your signs madden and trap me,
Your glances whip me to passion, my darling.

167

Often the peacock cries
And the hawk cuckoo calls,
My lover has not come
And the clouds gather.
Often the clouds thunder
And the lightning glitters,
My lover has not come
And the clouds gather.
My lover has not come
And my heart is scared
And the clouds gather.

A similar situation is expressed in Chinese poetry:

A great wind and darkness;
Day after day it is dark.
I lie awake, cannot sleep,
And gasp with longing.

Dreary, dreary the gloom;
The thunder growls.
I lie awake, cannot sleep,
And am destroyed with longing.[87]

168

Sāwan and the leaping, reeling rain
How the heart longs, O friend,
The peacock tweaks me with its cry
The frogs roar.
Sāwan and the leaping, reeling rain
How the heart longs, O friend,

The hawk whimpers
And the grasshoppers chirrup.
Sāwan and the leaping, reeling rain
How the heart longs, O friend,
In the streams and rivers
Water goes leaping.
Sāwan and the leaping, reeling rain
How the heart longs, O friend,
Gusts of wind
Scatter the drizzling rain
But yet my heart's thief does not come,
Sāwan and the leaping, reeling rain
How the heart longs, O friend.

169

"My bangle is broken, O friend,
Broken by my husband on the bed."
"Was it your father
Who gave you your bangle
Or was it a lover?"
"My bangle came neither
From father nor lover
But my kinswoman sent it
Through my husband's little sister.
My bangle is broken, O friend,
Broken by my husband on the bed."

BARSĀTĪ

170

August and a drizzling midnight,
I play at "twenty-fives" with my husband.
In a dish of gold I serve him food
But he does not eat.

Pachīsī or "twenty-fives" is a game played with seven cowries as
dice and so named from the highest throw which is twenty-five. Our
familiar Parcheesi was derived from this game.

171

Darling in the house you promised me
But where did you go for the night?
In a dish of gold I served your food
But you did not eat.

GRINDING SONGS
JATSĀR

Grinding is done by women in the early afternoon or in the later part of the night, at any time of the year; and as they grind, they sing to keep themselves from feeling lonely.[88]

172

With a seer of wheat
I went to the grinding-room,
Holding the peg the lovely girl
Weeps in the room.
The grindstone does not move
The peg does not move,
Holding the stone the lovely girl
Weeps in the room.
"O traveler on the path,
O my brother,
You are my well-wisher
Take with you this message,
Give this message to my husband—
Your wife weeps in the grinding-room."
Her husband is playing with dice
He goes and tells him
"Your wife weeps in the grinding-room."
To the trees he throws the dice
And hurries to the room
He picks her up
And puts her on his lap,

With his handkerchief he wipes her face.
Keep the handkerchief for your office
"O king, use my sari for my face."

173

I am only a little girl
How can I come on your bed?
My father was blind
And did not heed my age,
My mother and father
Are leaving me behind
How can I come on your bed?
I am only a little cucumber
And my waist is slender
How can I come on your bed?
My waist will be broken
How can I come on your bed?

NOTES

FOREWORD BY BARBARA STOLER MILLER

1. Biographical material has been supplied mainly by Mildred Archer, whose own account of her husband's career and their life in India appears as an essay, "A Passion for India," in the "Dr. W. G. Archer Memorial Number," *Roopa-Lekha* (1979–80), 51:17–21. After their marriage in 1934 Mildred lived in India, sharing her husband's work on Indian art and culture. Her own scholarship has focused on the artistic history of British India, but her knowledge of folk and court painting is also considerable. From 1954 to 1980 she was in charge of Prints and Drawings at the India Office Library, where she has published, among other works, several major catalogues of drawings and paintings—*Indian Natural History Drawings* (1962), *British Drawings* (1969), *Company Drawings* (1972), *Indian Popular Painting* (1977), *Indian Miniatures in the India Office Library* (with Toby Falk, 1981). Her recent publications include *India and British Portraiture, 1770–1825* (1979) and *Early Views of India: The Picturesque Journeys of Thomas and William Daniell, 1786–1794* (1980). W. G. Archer's Convocation Address delivered at the Punjab University in Chandigarh on July 27, 1968, when he was awarded an honorary doctorate, contains a brief personal memoir.

2. *Indian Popular Painting in the India Office Library* (London: Her Majesty's Stationery Office, 1977).

3. London: Allen and Unwin, 1935.

4. "Maithil Paintings," *Marg* (1949), 3(3):24–33. Archer's discovery of this painting was indirectly responsible for its revival in the 1960s under Indian Government patronage; see Mildred Archer, *Indian Popular Painting*, pp. 5, 6, 85–104; also Yves Vequaud, *The Woman Painters of Mithila* (London: Thames and Hudson, 1977); Pupul Jayakar, *The Earthen Drum* (Delhi: National Museum, 1981), pp. 92–119; Upendra Thakur, *Madhubani Painting* (Delhi: Abhinav, 1981).

5. See J. J. Meyer, *Sexual Life in Ancient India,* 2nd vol. (London: Routledge and Kegan Paul, 1930), ch. 3 "The Wedding." and A. S. Altekar, *The Position of Women in Hindu Civilization* (Varanasi: Motilal Banarsidass, 1956; reprint of 1938 ed.). Accounts of wedding rituals abound in the anthropol-

ogical literature; among recent studies that provide added comparative material for Archer's account, see Oscar Lewis, *Village Life in Northern India* (Urbana: University of Illinois Press, 1958), ch. 5, "The Marriage Cycle"; K. M. Kapadia, *Marriage and Family in India* (Bombay: Oxford University Press, 1958); Giri Raj Gupta, *Marriage, Religion, and Society in India* (New York: John Wiley, 1974); Doranne Jacobson, "Songs of Social Distance," *Journal of South Asian Literature* (1975), 11(1–2):45–60; J. Gabriel Campbell, *Saints and Householders: A Study of Hindu Ritual and Myth Among the Kangra Rajputs, Bibliotheca Himalayica,* ser. 3, vol. 6 (Kathmandu: Ratna Pustak Bhandar, 1976), ch. 3.B, "Marriage"; Ronald Inden and Ralph Nicholas, *Kinship in Bengali Culture* (Chicago: University of Chicago Press, 1977), ch. 2.1, "Marriage and Procreation"; Ruth and Stanley Freed, *Rites of Passage in Shantinagar, American Museum of Natural History Anthropological Papers* 56(3) (New York: American Museum of Natural History, 1980); Lina M. Fruzetti, *The Gift of a Virgin: Women, Marriage, and Ritual in Bengali Society* (New Brunswick: Rutgers University Press, 1982); Lynn Bennett, *Dangerous Wives and Sacred Sisters: Social and Symbolic Roles of High-caste Women in Nepal* (New York: Columbia University Press, 1983); Tom Selwyn, "Images of Reproduction: An Analysis of a Hindu Marriage Ceremony," *Man* (1979), N.S. 14:684–98. Archer's books on tribal culture also contain substantial material on marriage rituals and songs; see *The Blue Grove,* pp. 79–174; *The Hill of Flutes,* pp. 170–94, 222–71. For a survey of North Indian women's place in wider social contexts, see Doranne Jacobson and Susan S. Wadley, *Women in India: Two Perspectives* (Columbia, Mo.: South Asia Books, 1977); also the annotated bibliography *Women of South Asia: A Guide to Resources* by Carol Sakala (Millwood, N.Y.: Kraus, 1980).

6. *Indian Popular Painting,* 85–86.

7. Kayasths are a high-ranking Hindu caste whose male members were traditionally employed as scribes and accountants. According to various census reports, they are usually landholders and members of "learned professions," such as clerks, schoolteachers, and civil servants. See James and Nancy Duncan, "Residential Landscapes and Social Worlds," in *An Exploration of India: Geographical Perspectives on Society and Culture,* ed. by David E. Sopher (Ithaca: Cornell University Press, 1980), pp. 274–75.

8. See G. A. Grierson, *Linguistic Survey of India* 5(2) (Calcutta: Government Printing, 1903) (Indo-Aryan Family, Eastern Group—Specimens of Bihari and Oriya Languages), section on Bhojpuri; Udai Narain Tiwari, *The Origin and Development of Bhojpuri,* Asiatic Society Monograph Series 10 (Calcutta, 1960); Shaligram Shukla, *Bhojpuri Grammar* (Washington, D.C.: Georgetown University Press, 1981).

9. See Ruth Finnegan, *Oral Poetry: Its Nature, Significance, and Social Context* (Cambridge: Cambridge University Press, 1977).

10. Chandramani Singh, *Marriage Songs from Bhojpuri Region* (Jaipur: Kitab Mahal, 1979); Edward O. Henry, "North Indian Wedding Songs: The Analysis of Functions and Meanings," *Journal of South Asian Literature* (1975), 11(1–2):61–93; "The Variety of Music in a North Indian Village: Reassessing Cantometrics," *Ethnomusicology* (1976), 20(1):49–65; *Musical Culture of a North Indian Village* (San Diego: San Diego State University Press, 1984).

11. Henry, "Wedding Songs," pp. 84–89; Jacobson, "Songs of Social Distance."

12. A record of Bhojpuri music, "Chant the Names of God: Village Music from the Bhojpuri-speaking Area of India," is available from Edward O. Henry, Department of Anthropology, San Diego State University.

13. Archer's observations are theoretically amplified by the work of several anthropologists, e.g., Arnold van Gennep, *The Rites of Passage*, trans. by M. B. Vizedom and G. L. Caffee (Chicago: University of Chicago Press, 1960); Louis Dumont, "Marriage in India, the Present State of the Question," *Contributions to Indian Sociology*, 5(1961), 7(1964), 9(1966) and *Homo Hierarchicus* (Paris: Gallimard, 1966); Victor Turner, *The Ritual Process: Structure and Anti-Structure* (Chicago: Aldine, 1969) and *Dramas, Fields, and Metaphors: Symbolic Action in Human Society* (Ithaca: Cornell University Press, 1974). See also Suzanne Hanchett, "Recent Trends in the Study of Folk Hinduism and India's Folklore," *Journal of Indian Folkloristics* (1978), 1(1):40–54 (Mysore: Folklore Fellows of India).

AUTHOR'S PREFACE

1. [Editors' note: see Archer bibliography.]

2. L. S. S. O'Malley, revised by J. W. F. James, *Bihar and Orissa District Gazetteers: Shahabad*, 40 (Patna, 1924).

3. Ram Naresh Tripathi, *Kabita Kaumudī* (Hindi Mandir, Allahabad, no date).

4. London: G. P. Putnam, 1927.

5. In the Bhojpuri originals the form Gaurā sometimes occurs instead of the Sanskritic form Gaurī.

TEXT

1. Trans. by David Gascoigne (London: Faber and Faber, 1936).

2. Compare *Alice in Wonderland* and the *Just So Stories*. For an analysis of

Alice in Wonderland from this point of view see William Empson, *Some Versions of Pastoral* (London: Chatto, 1935), pp. 253–94.

3. For the peculiar validity of this term when applied to this stage of the marriage, see an article by Verrier Elwin, "I Married a Gond," *Man in India* (1940), 20.

4. See also W. Crooke, *Religion and Folklore of Northern India* (London: Humphrey Milford, 1926), p. 328, on the general phallic and fertilizing significance of rice pounders and mortars.

5. In Elizabethan imagery, earth symbolizes the virgin. Compare these lines from Middleton's *A Fair Quarrel:*

> Mine's yet
> A virgin earth; the worm hath not been seen
> To wriggle in her chaste bowels, and I'd be loth
> A gunpowder fellow should deflower her now.

6. Compare the phallic shrines of Shiva and bridal paintings in Mithila, e.g., Figure 2.

7. *Dūb* grass (*Cynodon dactylon*); *Kush,* or *Darbh,* grass (*Poa cynosuroides*); and *Munj* grass (*Saccharum munja*), by the fact that they can survive fire are also embles of longevity.

8. "The Great Russians are said to throw corn on the bride and bridegroom 'in order that their married life shall be fruitful'; and the Russian clerk or sexton who sprinkles hops on the bride's head wishes that she may be as fruitful as the plant. Addison wrote in the seventeenth century that among the Jews of some countries 'the Guests bring with them handfuls of corn, which they cast at the New Married, saying Increase and Multiply. By which they also wish them Peace and Abundance.' And the same custom is still practiced by West Russian Jews." Edward Westermarck, *The History of Human Marriage,* 3 vols. (London: MacMillan, 1921), 2:489.

9. William Cobbett in *Rural Rides* (London: Dent, 1934) notes how a good nut year is believed to involve a rise in illegitimate children.

10. A flat stone on which spices and condiments are crushed, used with a roller. It is called "curry-stone" to distinguish it from the grindstone used to grind foodgrains.

11. Ernest Jones in "The Theory of Symbolism," *Papers on Psycho-Analysis* (London: Ballière, 1938), p. 153, notes that Sophocles' Oedipus repeatedly speaks of "the mother-field from which I sprouted." Shakespeare makes Boult, on the point of deflowering the recalcitrant Marina, say: "An if she were a thornier piece of ground, than she is, she shall be ploughed." The

words for "plough" in Latin, Greek, and Oriental languages were customarily used also to denote the sexual act, and we still use such words as "seed," "fertility," "barrenness," for vegetation as well as for human beings. The association becomes quite manifest in the well-known fertilizing magic, a custom that lasted late into civilized times. It consisted in a naked pair performing the sexual act in the field, so as to encourage the latter to imitate their example. The Greek words for garden, meadow, field, common female symbols, were used also to denote the female genital organ.

12. See Crooke, *Religion and Folklore*, p. 404. A parallel form of symbolism is used by Binjhwars of the Central Provinces when a winnowing fan filled with rice is put in the marriage shed and a dagger is laid on it. The former represents the bride and the latter the bridegroom.

13. Havelock Ellis, in *Studies in the Psychology of Sex* (London/New York: Random House, 1936), 1:171, notes that "the mythology of Hawaii tells of goddesses who were impregnated, by bananas they had placed beneath their garments," and J. P. Mills in *The Rengma Nagas* (London: Macmillan, 1937), p. 78, states that "among the Rengma Nagas very few bananas are grown. They contain seeds and it is believed that if a woman swallows a seed by mistake she will produce a bastard."

14. J. Abbott, *The Keys of Power: A Study of Indian Ritual and Belief* (London: Methuen, 1932), pp. 299–300.

15. Compare the Book of Common Prayer's declaration of the causes for which matrimony was ordained: first, for the procreation of children, secondly for a remedy against sin and to avoid fornication, and thirdly for the mutual society, and help and comfort that the one ought to have of the other.

16. Compare the following passage from Middleton, *Women Beware Women:*

> How do you like him girl? This is your husband.
> Like him, or like him not, wench, you shall have him
> And you shall love him.

17. For an exposition of horoscopes and the principles behind their comparison see R. V. Russell and Hiralal, *The Tribes and Castes of the Central Provinces of India* (London, 1916), 3:255–79.

18. Curds, cow dung, and butter derive from the cow and the water buffalo which, as supporters of village life, are naturally associated with vitality. *Gūr* or country sugar is probably used as a corollary to curds, with which it is usually eaten; and just as curds may be eaten to increase the vitality of the bride and bridegroom, *gūr* may be added to sweeten their relations. Edward Westermarck, in *The History of Human Marriage*, 2:489, notes that

"among some of the Little Russians, on the return of bride and bridegroom from church, the bride's mother sprinkles the bridegroom three times with wheat and evergreen, puts some wool at his chest, offers him two cakes and smears his mouth three times with honey, saying, 'May your life become as sweet as the honey, may you become as rich as the sheep and as warm as the wool.' "

19. Wherever the word butter is used in the text, it refers to the clarified butter known as ghee.

20. As in English weddings where guests are invited to view the presents, this is also an occasion to impress and to make a display before the neighbors. [Editors' note: see Stanley Tambiah, "Dowry and Bridewealth and the Property of Women in South Asia," in *Dowry and Bridewealth,* ed. by Jack Goody and Stanley Tambiah, *Cambridge Papers in Social Anthropology,* No. 7 (1973), pp. 59–169; also J. L. Comaroff, ed., *The Meaning of Marriage Payments* (New York: Academic Press, 1980).]

21. The object of washing the feet at this and other stages of the marriage is to rid the body of any evil spirit or pollution that may have been gathered on the way.

22. Camphor, for decontaminating purposes.

23. *Bukwā,* a paste made from water, *haldī,* and mustard oil. *Haldī* or turmeric through its yellow color—the color of ripe grain—is associated with the Mother Goddess and with fertility generally.

24. *Devas*—the gods of Hindu scriptures; as distinct from *deotās*—the petty gods of the countryside.

25. The hand-marks given on the mother's back and also on the walls of the bridal room are probably intended as a form of protection.

26. Pounding rice in a mortar is a disguised way of referring to intercourse. Compare a Holi song from the Gonds of Mandla, Central Provinces:

> Where does the oil-press come from?
> Whose is the pestle?
> Fie on you, boy
> My sex is the mortar
> Your stick is the pestle
> All day the breasted ox goes round—

(Verrier Elwin and Shamrao Hivale, *Folk Songs of the Maikal Hills* [Bombay: Oxford University Press, 1944], p. 336).

27. Alice M. Stevenson in *The Rites of the Twice-born* (London: Oxford

University Press, 1920), p. 61, compares the erection of the wedding canopy
to the reading of the banns for the last time in England. Both show that the
wedding is now imminent.

28. Crooke notes that "Kalars in the Central Provinces, before a wedding
procession starts, perform a curious rite known as 'marrying the well.' The
mother or aunt of the bridegroom goes to the well, sits with her legs dangling
down inside it, and asks what the bridegroom will give her. He goes round
the well seven times and a piece of koos grass is thrown into it at each turn.
Afterwards he promises her a present and she returns home." (W. Crooke,
Religion and Folklore, p. 64.)

29. Gaurī is worshipped since she is one of the seven ideal wives and can
endow the worshiper with unceasing good luck, Ganesh because his worship
also brings a good beginning. The dual form may be simply represented by a
handful of cow dung pressed into a cylindrical shape, known as *Gaurī-Ga-nesh*, or by two separate shapes.

30. The object of the hats is to protect the head from evil influences.

31. Rimming the eyes with black kohl and giving an iron case are both
for warding off evil spirits—the color black being feared by *bhūts* because it
is a death color.

32. This consists of touching the stone roller on some paddy tied in the
sari and then brandishing it around his head three times. Some cow dung is
then made up into a ball, passed round his head three times, and thrown
behind his back.

33. Westermarck gives similar examples of sympathetic magic at weddings
and notes for example that among some Southern Slavs a bowl of milk and
two spoons are put into the nuptial room "in order that the couple shall have
beautiful children." In Estonia the bridegroom's attendant cuts a small piece
off a whole loaf, butters it, and puts it in the bride's mouth; her children
will then have a small smooth mouth. In the same country, when the bride
is fetched in, she must wear no chains or bells, but be led in in solemn
silence; then she will have quiet children. (E. Westermarck, *The History of
Human Marriage*, 2:487.)

34. So called after the Doms, members of a sweeper caste who are noto-rious for their noisy abuse.

35. For a similar practice among Gadarias, compare Russell and Hiralal,
Tribes and Castes, 3:5. "While the bridegroom's party is absent at the bride's
house, the women who remain behind enjoy amusements of their own. One
of them strips herself naked, tying up her hair like a religious mendicant
and is known as Baba or holy father. In this state, she romps with her
companions in turn, while the others laugh and applaud."

36. Crooke (*Religion and Folklore*, p. 321) suggests that the stone is introduced as an emblem of stability.

37. The rice is a substitute for the ancestors, and in hiding the rice they confine the ancestors.

38. Syce (*sāis*) means a groom or horsekeeper; there is no pun on bridegroom in this word as there would seem to be in English.

39. In Northumberland, it was formerly customary for a bridal pair, as they rode to church, to be saluted by volleys of firearms at every farmhouse they passed, on the way. (*Country Folklore* [London: Folklore Society, 1926], 4:92.)

40. Mustard from its hot taste is believed to consume evil influences.

41. The object of the veiling like that of the marriage hat is to ward off evil spirits and the evil eye.

42. Crooke (p. 305) notes that in the standard ritual of *hāthleva* (hand seizing) the bridegroom grasps the bride's hand so as to include all her fingers in his own, as well as the thumb, the latter being most important as it ensures the birth of a son. A parallel use of the thumb is seen in the English nursery rhyme:

> I had a little husband
> No bigger than my thumb
> I put him in a pint pot
> And there I bade him drum.

43. Crooke (pp. 54–55) suggests that the function of the water is to purge the couple of their unmarried state.

44. This is a form of joke. Among Kurmis, "if the girls wish to have a joke, they take one of the bridegroom's shoes which he has left outside the house, wrap it up in a piece of cloth and place it on a shelf or in a cupboard, where the family god would be kept, with two lamps burning before it. Then they say to the bridegroom, 'Come and worship your household god'; and if he goes and does reverence to it they unwrap the cloth and show him his own shoe and laugh at him." (Russell and Hiralal, 4:61–66.)

45. Normally the male eats first and the woman eats what he leaves.

46. Among Kayasths of the Central Provinces an image of a cow is brought and the bridegroom pierces its nostrils with a little stick of gold. (Russell and Hiralal, 3:419.) There is a similar practice among Lohārs of the United Provinces. Crooke notes that "At a *Lohār* wedding an image of a fish made with flour is held by the bride which the bridegroom must pierce with an arrow while she tries to prevent him from doing so by moving it about, and

he refuses to enter the house till he succeeds—an obvious form of fertility magic which also appears in early Brahmanical ritual." (Crooke, p. 378.)

47. As in seventeenth-century England, this weeping is partly formal. Compare Robert Herrick, *An Epithalamie to Sir Thomas Southwell and his Ladie:*

> These Precious-Pearly-Purling teares,
> But spring from ceremonious feares,
> And 'tis but Native shame,
> That hides the loving flame:
> And may a while controule
> The soft and am'rous soule;
> But yet, love's fire will wast
> Such bashfulnesse at last.
> Then away; come, Hymen, guide
> To the bed, the bashfull Bride.

48. Compare the use of 'i' in T. S. Eliot's

> And let their liquid siftings fall
> To stain the stiff dishonoured shroud.

49. Arthur Waley, *The Book of Songs* (London: Allen and Unwin, 1937), p. 326.

50. *Gānjā* is a narcotic preparation made from the dried flowers of a tall bushy plant *(Canabis indica)* with flowers like a French marigold. The dried flowers are crushed and mixed with tobacco in equal parts. The mixed pellet of *gānjā* and tobacco is then put into a chilam. A lighted coal is added and the smoke inhaled. It is said to induce at first a feeling of energy but later a kind of mad blankness. *Bhāng* is a narcotic preparation made from the leaves of a sister plant to *gānjā (Canabis sativa)*. The sprigs of dried leaves are powdered and made up into a drink by mixing them with almonds, sugar, milk, and water. It is said to give a feeling of hilarity and elation. [Editor's note: *Canabis sativa* is, of course, the familiar marijuana plant.]

51. Russell and Hiralal, 1:302–4. [Editors' note: See also Wendy O'Flaherty, *Asceticism and Eroticism in the Mythology of Śiva* (London: Oxford University Press, 1973); Stella Kramrisch, *The Presence of Śiva* (Princeton: Princeton University Press, 1982).]

52. Verrier Elwin, *The Baiga* (London: Murray, 1939), p. 247.

53. Arthur Waley, *The Book of Songs,* p. 53.

54. Westermarck, 2:466.

55. E. W. Lane, *Arabian Society in the Middle Ages,* quoted in Havelock Ellis, *Studies in the Psychology of Sex.*

56. Ballad of Kanka and Līlā, *Eastern Bengal Ballads: Mymensingh,* trans. by Dinesh Chandra Sen (Calcutta, 1923–32), 1:218.

57. Crooke, p. 412.

58. *Garcia Lorca: Poems,* trans. by Stephen Spender and J. L. Gili (London: The Dolphin, 1939), p. 103.

59. J. P. Mills, *The Ao Nagas* (London: Macmillan, 1926), p. 270.

60. For yet another use of the fish image, compare P'ing Mei, *The Golden Lotus,* trans. by Clement Egerton, 4 vols. (London: Routledge, 1939), ch. 91. "The young couple became husband and wife that same night and enjoyed each other as fishes enjoy water."

61. Arthur Waley, *170 Chinese Poems* (London: Constable, 1918), p. 119.

62. Translated as *The Ocean of Love* by E. B. Eastwick (London, 1867), ch. 59.

63. [Editors' note: See Doranne Jacobson, "Songs of Social Distance: Women's Music in Central India," *Journal of South Asian Literature* (1975), 2:45–59.]

64. Verrier Elwin, *The Baiga,* p. 440.

65. Devendra Satyarthi, "Song-harvest from the Pathan Country," *The Modern Review* (October 1935).

66. Dinesh Chandra Sen, *Eastern Bengal Ballads: Mymensingh,* 1:112.

67. Devendra Satyarthi, "Song-harvest from the Pathan Country," *The Modern Review* (December 1935).

68. Dinesh Chandra Sen, *Eastern Bengal Ballads: Mymensingh,* 1:160.

69. Westermarck, 2:520.

70. A menstruating woman is ceremonially impure and is not allowed to cook food, do *pūjā,* or touch any pot with drinking water in it. She will also not wash, comb her hair, or change her dress until the period is over.

71. Evil spirits consist of men who have died unnatural deaths *(bhūt).* A death within twelve days of giving birth to a child is unnatural. Death by drowning is unnatural. Death by a wild animal is unnatural. Death by falling is unnatural. It is currently believed that the ghosts of women who have died in childbirth *(churails)* haunt a pregnant woman and are particularly dangerous at times of childbirth and at night. In the villages where houses rarely have latrines and easing takes place in the fields, a pregnant woman tries to relieve herself at twilight—before it is completely dark—in order to lessen the risks from *churails.*

72. Mother-in-law.

73. Verrier Elwin, *The Baiga*, p. 182. There is a detailed account by Shamrao Hirale in "The Dewar-Bhaiyi Relationship," *Man in India*, 23:157–67.

74. To avoid wearing them when impure.

75. Sympathetic actions to make the birth easier.

76. Iron—to ward off evil spirits, the idea being that "the fairies and elves of Europe, the *bhūt* of India, are creatures of the Stone Age surviving to a later time and entertaining a great hatred for the new metal which brought their kingdom to an end." Verrier Elwin, *The Agaria* (Bombay: Oxford University Press, 1942), p. 135. For a full discussion of the magic qualities of iron, see *The Agaria*, ch. 4.

77. To assist the womb in settling.

78. Crooke (pp. 98–99) notes that "The door stands in relation to the house as the boundary does to the village, marking off the domains of the friendly house-spirits within from those of the hostile spirits outside."

79. A germicide.

80. Pure in the sense that she is freed from the impurity of the confinement room. This room is impure because, during the twelve days, the mother is not allowed to go out and has to relieve herself in the room. The midwife sleeps in the room and cleans it. In poorer families she stays until the sixth day and is then replaced by other women of the house. In families that are better off, she stays all the twelve days, waiting on the mother, rubbing her with oil and keeping the room tidy. Until this impure room has been vacated and cleaned, the house itself is impure, and so long as the house is impure, a feast cannot take place.

81. Arthur Waley, *The Book of Songs*, p. 43.

82. Ibid., p. 79.

83. Shamrao Hivale and Verrier Elwin, *Songs of the Forest: The Folk Poetry of the Gonds* (London: Allen and Unwin, 1935), p. 124. A Gond *dadaria*.

84. A Pardhan *dadaria*, translated by Shamrao Hivale and Verrier Elwin.

85. Pardhan love song from the Maikal Hills, translated by Shamrao Hivale and Verrier Elwin.

86. There is a full discussion of the Hindu months and their English equivalents in Verrier Elwin, *Folk-songs of Chhattisgarh* (Delhi: Oxford University Press, 1946), pp. 433–36.

87. Arthur Waley, *The Book of Songs*, p. 93.

88. For an account of Marathi grinding songs, with a note on "the grinding situation," see Mary L. B. Fuller in *The New Review*, Calcutta (May/June 1940).

NEO-CONFUCIAN STUDIES

MODERN ASIAN LITERATURE SERIES

TRANSLATIONS FROM THE ORIENTAL CLASSICS

STUDIES IN ORIENTAL CULTURE

COMPANIONS TO ASIAN STUDIES

INTRODUCTION TO ORIENTAL CIVILIZATIONS
WM. THEODORE DE BARY, EDITOR